Alfred Lunt and Lynn Fontanne in *The Taming of the Shrew.*

PLAY PRODUCTION FOR AMATEURS

By

EMANUEL D. SCHONBERGER
Director of the Dakota Playmakers
University of North Dakota

THOMAS NELSON AND SONS
NEW YORK · · · · · · · · · 1938

COPYRIGHT, 1938
BY THOMAS NELSON AND SONS

PRINTED IN THE UNITED STATES OF AMERICA

CONTENTS

v

59496

PREFACE

This book is planned for use in Play Production, and as a handy manual for directors of amateur plays.

There are diversified opinions as to the objective of a school course in dramatics. One teacher says he trains actors for the stage, another pretends to develop appreciative auditors, a third attempts to prepare amateur play directors, and a fourth offers culture and appreciation of stage arts. This text concentrates on none of these aims, but tries to present material so that each instructor can achieve his individual goal.

The writer is convinced that there are excellent opportunities in colleges, schools, and communities for directors of amateur plays. For this reason, the director's point of view is stressed throughout the book. It should be particularly useful in colleges in which high school directors are trained as well as for the high school teacher himself. Each phase of the subject is presented in a separate chapter as a distinct project, and as concisely as possible. The student is expected to have access to plays and other library facilities, and to spend much time on practical assignments. Each chapter may be regarded as a unit, to be emphasized, subordinated, or entirely omitted, according to the plans of the instructor. Thus, if the purpose is mainly instruction in acting, all of Part One should be read for background, while Chapters VI, VII, and VIII would be used as a basis for the major part of the course. The several chapters in Part Two may be treated theoretically or practically, according to the instructor's preference.

The objection has been raised that it is a waste of time to try to teach women to use hammer and saw. The same objection may be raised in regard to trying to teach men to use needle and thread. Fortunately, all students in a class need not become expert in all the crafts. A woman may learn how a flat is made, without building it herself. The same is true of painting, lighting, costume and make-up. At least, everyone interested in the theatre should be eager for a thorough knowledge of costuming as an art.

Part Two may be used in a kind of division-of-labor way. While one set of students is working on projects for which they have a special aptitude, another group may work on an entirely different phase of stage craft. All students should be required to pass an examination on the theory of all the arts.

Where so many sources contribute to a book, it is difficult to give specific credit. Among others, the following authorities have been consulted for information and confirmation: Lee Simonson, Harold Helvenston, Philip Barber, Stark Young, Halliam Bosworth, John Dolman, Clarence Stratton, Milton Smith, Andre Smith, Louis Hartman, A. M. Drummond, Sheldon Cheney, Sellman and Selden, Clayton Hamilton, William Archer, George Pierce Baker, and the Theatre Guild.

The most vital source of inspiration and enthusiasm for the theatre is the memory of the work of such artists as Sarah Bernhardt, Ada Rehan, Henry

Irving, Joseph Jefferson, Richard Mansfield, Mrs.
Fiske, E. H. Sothern, Julia Marlowe, the Barry-
mores, Otis Skinner, William Gillette, as well as
those new artists who mark a decidedly agreeable
change in the style of acting and design.

E. D. SCHONBERGER
University of North Dakota
Grand Forks, North Dakota

INTRODUCTION

"A well-ordered stage is an ornament to society, an incentive to wit and learning, and a school of refinement and virtue."—Lord Chesterfield.

Our commercial stage has not always been a "well-ordered" stage. It naturally shaped itself for material rewards rather than for cultural values. The amateur stage differs in that it can adapt itself perfectly to the tastes of the community in which it thrives.

Thanks to the alert publisher, who makes good plays instantly available to the reading public, and to the far-sighted educator, who has admitted dramatics into the school curriculum as an unquestioned educational force, we can now have Lord Chesterfield's well-ordered stage in our own hands. Our effectively organized amateur movement has placed the stage on an entirely different basis. Having no profit motive, it concerns itself with the purely artistic and cultural, and being more or less subsidized, it can afford to be experimental. It touches intimately our young people, some of whom develop into playwrights, designers, directors, actors. Best of all, as our professional theatre folk like to believe, these youngsters constitute an educated audience for the legitimate theatre of the future.

Actors produce spiritual values that far transcend many of the material needs of a community. Men do not live by bread alone. The farmer may be glad to produce the bread in exchange for what the artist can give him of inspiration, of pleasure, and of a glimpse of a broader horizon of life.

Today amateur performances are not dull. Young people in schools and colleges are learning to act together as they have always known how to sing together. A well-directed amateur play is inspiring to the performers, and to the audience. These apprentice actors bring to the stage a simplicity, spontaneity, and a naive zest that are far more pleasant than the studied efforts of some professional actors, who have no flair for their work.

Best of all, the amateur theatre gives the community a focus of attention, which it can contemplate and approve, and in which a common interest and pride are shared.

But let us see what play-acting can do for student actors. It offers a more intimate acquaintance with dramatic literature than a mere reading or class analysis could possibly give, and by identifying themselves with the characters, they absorb the social import of the play, learn a good deal about the springs of human behavior, and the elemental passions, as well as the cultivated emotions, of the race. Through a short two hours' traffic on the stage, the young student may live a crowded life-time of experience, a richness of physical, mental, and spiritual action and re-action which his own circumstances might never yield.

Acting is one of the best methods of training in speech and in public speaking. The modern standard of reading and speaking is the conversational standard. Dramatic dialogue, particularly that of the modern vintage, is pure conversation. As such, it is easily spoken with the ease and vocal flexibility that belong to conversation. In learning to adapt his style to these elements, the student gradually loses those distressing declamatory tendencies that he has, almost invariably, acquired. The simple, spontaneous style of speech, developed in a well-coached and well-performed play, carries over into activities where temptations to indirect, oratorical insincerity are more subtle.

Acting is a valuable exercise in mental concentration. In order to be effective on the stage, a student must attend to the business in hand. In reading his lines, he must keep his mind focused on what has been said, on what he is saying in reply, and on what is to be said in consequence of what he is now saying. Drama is a matter of cause and effect. The speech of one actor is the cause of the speech of another, so the student player must listen intently and think alertly while the episode progresses. This calls for almost as thorough concentration as a problem in science, with the added advantage that it encourages the student to self-expression.

Self-respect and self-confidence are developed through dramatics more quickly than through any other school activity. In coping with his fellows on the stage, and with an audience in front of him, the timid student gradually loses his shyness, acquiring control of himself and of his means of expression. He learns to submerge himself in his role, to vitalize and project this other self across the footlights, and to enjoy a sensation of personal power. He acquires a mental, emotional, and physical balance that will be immensely valuable to him in the social and business relations of his later life.

The stage is in the hands of our school people once more. The sincere director can be a vital, constructive force in the community.

Part One
THE PERSONAL ARTS

CHAPTER I

APPROACH TO PLAY PRODUCTION

Before a student can hope to take part in dramatics intelligently he must understand the nature of drama, and must have at least a bird's-eye view of its history. He must know something of dramatic literature in general, and a good deal about the construction of a play. Without a knowledge of his dramatic heritage, the student is bound to be a superficial actor, and extremely limited as a director. The best way to succeed in a game of any kind is to learn all there is to know about it first. The student who wants to succeed in play making will be genuinely interested in storing away all the knowledge possible against his future needs.

What Is Drama?—Clayton Hamilton defines a play clearly and simply thus: "A *play* is a story *devised* to be *presented* by *actors* on a *stage* before an *audience*." The italicized words indicate the elements in play production. *Story* suggests the nature of the content. It is not an essay, or a sermon. It may achieve the purpose of either, or both directly, but in substance it is the account of experiences of a group of imagined people. *Devised* implies the special technique that sets drama apart from other literary forms. *Presented* means a play is really not a play until it has been performed. *Stage* defines the place of production. By *actors* is indicated the skilled human agents through whose speech and behavior on the stage the story

3

Before an audience points out the sole aim of a play.

This definition covers every detail of the composite art of the theatre. It excludes all controversy as to what constitutes a play, and applies to the drama of every age and nation. It puts no restrictions upon the playwright or producer, but amply allows for any new effect either is clever enough to invent.

Classification.—Every playwright's purpose is to move the audience emotionally, and his secondary motive is to move them in a particular way. This secondary purpose forms the basis of the classification of plays into four general types, tragedy, comedy, melodrama, farce. To be sure, many variations may be played on these four. Polonius had a dozen hyphenated types at his tongue's end. But for purposes of play production an accurate understanding of the differences between these types is quite adequate and altogether indispensable.

Tragedy is a serious picture of strong or weak characters struggling more or less heroically against obstacles that prove unsurmountable in the end. The characters are more important than the story into which they are fitted. The plot grows out of their strength or weakness.

Comedy is akin to tragedy in that the characters are of first importance, and that the story shapes itself to their peculiarities. The comic situation is based upon the foibles of society held up to be laughed at, rather than wept over as in tragedy. In the performance, comedy calls for the same careful attention to characterization and motive as does tragedy, but comedy proceeds with a light heart

The Terrace Garden Theatre in Yankton College.

and a buoyant step. The best comedy is a genuinely serious study of the funny quirks in human nature.

Melodrama makes the plot so important that the characters need be little more than figureheads. It is satisfied with general stage types: hero; heroine; villain; ingenue; etc. These line up on opposite sides of some moral fence across which they fight for mastery with passionate seriousness, as in tragedy. But the villain is invariably foiled, and the hero is freed to marry the heroine and live happily ever after. Melodrama moves with sweeping momentum toward a calamity that is happily averted at the end.

Farce, like melodrama, is a plot play in which the characters may be normal human beings or grotesque distortions, while the situations may border on the impossibly ridiculous. Farce is naturally played with artistically restrained abandon.

Development of Drama.—Reformers of every era have worried over the condition of their theatre, and over the quality of plays written and produced. But the breath of time has blown away the chaff, and the plays that remain have permanent and vital value. With these we may compare our own output in an attempt to decide which of our plays bear the imprint of permanency, and why.

It may be interesting to note how the physical aspect of the stage, on which the play is performed, influences the playwright's technique. The Greek open-air theatre was a place of magnificent distances. The language and impression had to carry over vast areas of open auditorium. Vocal modulations and subtle facial expression were lost. Instinctively, therefore, playwrights employed the diction of highest sound values. To enhance expression actors wore exaggerated masks to project emotion and amplify tone. Resounding speech was the dramatist's best medium. The nature of the Greek stage therefore determined the style of composition. Scholars have called it the drama of Rhetoric.

Elizabethan drama, partly from the nature of the stage and partly by imitation, fell into much the same pattern. In his prologue to *Tamburlaine*, Christopher Marlowe promised his prospective audience a story told in "high-astounding terms."

As the stage began to portray actual contemporary conditions, and as the distance between footlights and audience was lessened, dialogue began to approach the ideal of actual speech. Taking a hint from John Fletcher and ignoring John Dryden, the work of the later Restoration dramatists—Congreve, Farquhar, Vanbrugh, Wycherly—began to contain more and more the essence of colloquial speech. Sheridan and Goldsmith carried it a step further. These men wrote as they heard people talk, somewhat verbosely and ornamentally perhaps, but still after the manner of polite conversation. Thus, the stage again exerted its influence to bring about what has been called the Drama of Conversation.

About the middle of the last century, civilization took a still more practical turn. The spirit of scientific inquiry invaded every phase of life, making its impression on literature, philosophy, religion. Dramatists suddenly lost their taste for playing with life, and began to deal with it seriously. As theatres multiplied, they grew smaller and more intimate. Stage settings began to assume the semblance of actual environment. Playwrights responded to this innovation with plays of fine, or gross, realism. Because modern drama attempts to represent life as it actually is, the drama of today has been called the Drama of Illusion.

At the moment, realism has lost much of its original force. Playwrights are completely unsettled in their points of view. Never has drama been so widely studied as now, and students of the theatre are constantly seeking new ideas, or combinations of new and old, in a hectic effort to devise something to fit the tempo of our mechanical age.

Form Versus Substance.—The form, or the technique of play construction, is of subordinate importance. We have seen the unities of time, place, and action, violated by Shakespeare and others, and we have seen them strictly observed, with equally good effect, by followers of the *well-made* model. Today Charles Rann Kennedy packs a tremendous lot of genuine drama into one interior, into one unbroken unit of time, and into one classically surveyed line of action in his *Servant In The House.* On the other hand, Marc Connelly's *The Green Pastures* makes as many deviations from the narrow path as Shakespeare's *Anthony and Cleopatra,* and with excellent results.

The stuff drama is made of is more interesting than the mold into which it may be forced. The Greek tragedies of 500 B.C. are readily fitted into a modern stage setting, but the philosophy of life out of which they are spun is alien to the modern mind. Our mental and emotional patterns are not so easily adjustable as our architectural tastes. The historically minded student may watch a Greek tragedy with as much delight as a musician listening to classical music, but the modern theatre audience cannot be blamed for lack of enthusiasm over a play so entirely foreign to their interests and emotional experience.

The motivating force of all social progress is struggle. Any kind of struggle, at any given time, suggests to the playwright the kind of conflict he may utilize to advantage in his plays. Social drama has its roots in social injustice, and a good play is an experiment in adjustment. As society becomes more complex, points of contention become more numerous. This gives our dramatist a much wider field than in any previous era. This is particularly true where freedom of speech gives him a free rein. The surviving Greek plays show a surprisingly narrow range. The Elizabethan spread over a slightly wider area. Our scope is limitless.

"All the world loves a lover." This is another way of saying that the struggle for adjustment between the sexes is an eternal dramatic theme, as old as the Garden of Eden, and as new as the latest rivalry for a fraternity pin.

Any play great enough to survive its original run must touch life at the source. The greatest stage hits of any age are liable to pass out of the picture with the day that applauded them. These catch only a transient phase. *Of Thee I Sing* is a good example. The popular playwright meets his audience on their own ground, within their own sphere of immediate mental and emotional experience. The great playwright digs down into the roots of life.

Modern drama is a serious examination of social forces in action. It may oppose woman to some form of masculine tyranny (Ibsen). It may pit man against the onrush of feminism (Strindberg). It may make an independent personality snap its fingers in the face of convention (Shaw). It may encourage an enlightened conscience to defy the bigotry of some hypocritical creed (Jones). It may array the weak against the strong (Galsworthy). Or, it may concern itself entirely with elemental sex struggles (O'Neill).

Change in Technique.—The well-made play invented by Scribe, and perfected by Ibsen, may have been hard to write, but it was easy to produce. It eliminated the trouble and expense of multiple sets of scenery, and was popular for about fifty years. This model might be in greater vogue today if it were not for the screen, with its greater freedom of technique.

Shortly after 1900, dramatists returned to the multiple-scene models. One by one playwrights began to violate the established *unities*. Knoblauch's *My Lady's Dress*, Drinkwater's *Abraham Lincoln*, O'Neill's *Emperor Jones* are early examples. Encouraged by improved facilities—the elevator stage, the revolving stage, the wagon stage, and the cyclorama—playwrights launched out on bolder projects. Shaw's *Back To Methuselah* starts at 6,000 B.C. and continues up to some 30,000 A.D., Connelly's *Green Pastures* takes us all over God's heaven and the green earth below. Tired of everyday surroundings, dramatists are ransacking history. Anderson gives us *Elizabeth The Queen, Mary Of Scotland, Valley Forge, The Wingless Victory*. Besier shows us the *Barretts Of Wimpole Street*. Then there are *Allison's House, Pride and Prejudice, Jane Eyre*, all successfully staged. Our dramatic traditions are so unsettled that no one can predict what will appear tomorrow. We are still experimenting with all phases of the stage arts. We have tried elaborate settings, and are now simplifying. We have adopted, and dismissed, all kinds of *isms*. Acting, too, has achieved a simplicity that would have made even David Garrick, an exponent of simple diction, say: "If you are right, then I was all wrong."

How to Study a Play.—In the preceding pages, we have examined the play as a form of literary expression. In later chapters we will learn how to prepare the environment in which the play may come to life. Now, as potential actors, we are to learn how to realize a thing of beauty and power out of the dead mass of conventional symbols inscribed between the pages of a book.

Before we can hope to act a play effectively, we must learn how to read it intelligently. A play is the product of the playwright's imagination. If it is to be re-born in the mind of the student, it must be by the same route. If we are inexperienced in reading plays, the study of drama may be just another dose of dull drudgery. But if we have trained ourselves to realize, and to visualize as we read, the seemingly prosaic lines of dialogue begin to stir with life. We begin to see an interesting variety of people moving about, and to hear them talk in a life-like variety of tones and speech mannerisms. If we concentrate on the picture, and turn our imaginations free, we shall be living with them, identifying ourselves with one or another of them, fighting on the side of our favorites, thrilling to their predicaments, and exulting in their triumphs. The right way to read a play is with the imagination.

We must first get a clear picture of the setting, even if we have to draw a rough sketch of it. Where is the action laid? Is it an interior? An exterior? What kind? We get a clear impression of the essential details. If it is an interior set, we get a picture of the walls, the positions of doors and windows, the furniture used, anything that may tell us something of the people we are to meet presently. When we have clearly visualized the environment, we begin to look for the folk who are to enliven it. Who appears first, and why? In what direction do the speeches point; to what has already happened, or to what is about to happen?

In this way we read the play through, episode by episode. We note at what point in the sequence of events the curtain rises. In every good play, much must have happened before we are let in as witnesses. It is stimulating to note how this necessary preliminary information is dealt out; how it links up with what is to come; how the play gradually gathers momentum, drawing in more and more people, important and otherwise; how, and where, it reaches its peak of intensity; and finally, how quickly it resolves itself into a conclusion.

We are aware of any devices the author may have used to capture and hold our interest. We mark his method of letting the characters reveal themselves to us through speech and action. We note the type of conflict on which the plot is based. This is particularly important to the actor, as it suggests the emotional attitude he must maintain throughout the play.

Divisions of the Play.—In Julius Caesar's time, Gaul was divided into three parts. This was an arbitrary political partition, but many things that have existence in time and space are, by their very nature, divided into three parts at least: a beginning, a middle, and an end. This is true of any well constructed play. Some scholars, however, have divided a play into five parts: exposition, rising action, climax, falling action, and conclusion. Whether these *logical divisions,* as they have been named, are of any technical value to the playwright or the critic, they are very helpful to the student in analyzing the action.

Before we attempt to examine these logical divisions, we must disassociate them in our minds from the Mechanical Divisions, the acts and scenes. The blocking out of a play into acts may be as arbitrary as sub-dividing Gaul. It may be a simple provision for the relief of actor or audience; it may be a necessary shift in the environment; or it may represent lapse of time. Older drama shows a surprising uniformity in this respect: five acts, sub-divided variously into scenes. Modern drama favors three acts, although four, and even five acts are still to be found.

The playwright's chief concern in planning his acts is to have a strong *curtain.* He must stir the audience sufficiently to hold their interest over the intermission. To a large extent, the success of a play depends upon these mechanical divisions. A long first act is sure to be boresome. A long last act is certain to be fatal. The psychological effect of scene and act is so pronounced that it calls for careful planning on the part of the writer, as well as of the director and actor.

Unlike the mechanical divisions, the logical divisions have no external form to mark them off from one another. The author of a good play may not even have been conscious of them when he wrote. But, if his work is logically constructed these divisions are fairly easy to trace.

Exposition.—This preliminary step is just what the word implies, an explanation of the conditions on which the play is based. It sets forth all details needed to a clear understanding of the action, and tells what has already happened. It introduces the important characters, suggests the difficulties these characters are to encounter, and raises questions that demand to be answered.

This information must all be given to the audience *indirectly.* They are not to suspect that they are being informed. Exposition tells everything, but must appear to tell nothing. Someone, in a position to know, must tell it to another, who is as much of a stranger to the situation as the audience. Our first question is whether the exposition is spontaneous, natural, and indirect. Does the information we need simply "leak out" through the conversation we are privileged to overhear? It is very important that the student actor recognize this veiled purpose of the exposition. The actor, who is to receive the information, asks questions the audience would ask, and the one responding must send that information, *through* his partner on the stage, *to* the auditors.

Before the exposition is finished the motivating force must make itself felt. This may be any element that threatens to disturb the harmony, and to which the character will react in such a way as to forward the plot. In Kennedy's *Servant In The House,* it is the drains. In Archer's *Green Goddess,* it is news of the condemned prisoners. In many good plays, bits of exposition may recur throughout the several acts, but the important details must be given at the outset.

Rising Action.—When we begin to feel that "something must be done about this," rising action has started, and the plot has been fully launched. From this point, the various forces begin to drive, and the conflict acquires momentum, which rises steadily to a point of highest intensity. During this rise, characters must be actuated by motives made clear to the audience at once, or at a carefully considered point. Pre-modern playwrights never left the audience in doubt for a moment. Shakespeare always told the audience in advance, and, often, not once, but three times. He took the audience into his confidence. The characters on the stage might be fooled into thinking the villain was a saint, and a saint the villain, but the audience knew him for what he was every step of the way.

It was this superior knowledge the audience shared with the author that gave the old-fashioned melodrama such a punch. It gave the audience a chance to take sides violently for, or against, to follow the hero with passionate interest, and the villain with hissing hatred. They enjoyed this partisanship immensely. With the advent of our mystery play, this rule went largely into the discard. Formerly the playwright worked *with* the audience *against* the characters on the stage. The new technique keeps everyone guessing.

Climax.—The definition of climax is ladder, but we have come to think of the word as meaning the highest rung of the ladder. In a play, a figurative ladder is set up against a figurative wall. On the other side there is something startling to be seen. The audience takes pleasure in climbing this ladder for the sake of that satisfying peep over the top. Each added rung is just so much added tension and suspense.

The climax may mark a sudden reversal in the fortunes of war, or a startling revelation of character. A force, that has been in abeyance during the rise, now may assert itself. The tension snaps, and the action is ready to travel down hill to resolve itself into the inevitable consequences.

Falling Action.—The modern dramatist has wisely shortened the distance between the climax and the *denouement.* Still, he must take a little time to disentangle the threads of his plot. In the old five act play, the falling action was leisurely. Audiences were more patient than now.

There is a point in every play where the tension is relieved, and the suspense satisfied. From this point the situation must swiftly draw to a logical conclusion. It is important that the actor appreciate the effect of this upon the audience. Up to this time he has worked to keep the audience keyed up, and eager for the great event of the play. Now he is to let them down easily, soothe their harried feelings, and send them home to the ordinary tasks of life. When the long drawn out falling action cannot be avoided, the ingenious play-wright resorts to a trick called the final suspense. He introduces something that deceives the audience into thinking that their guess as to the outcome has been wrong. Thus temporarily curious about the new element, they are willing to wait for the natural resolution of the plot.

Denouement.—The outcome of the play should leave the impression of finality. In classic tragedy this was called the catastrophe, which means literally the final turning point, but which technically implies the deaths of the protagonists. In Shakespeare's tragedies all of the best people were killed off. In modern serious plays the rule is not rigid. Ibsen's Hedda Gabler dies by her own hand, but his Nora only leaves her husband. For this reason

Courtesy, Theatre Guild.

From Porgy and Bess.

perhaps *A Doll's House* would not classify as true tragedy, but it certainly develops on tragic lines and would be played in that mood.

The denouement in melodrama is a happy surprise. In comedy it may be a joyful joining of hostile hands, or a pointed rebuke. In farce it may be any kind of ridiculous adjustment. In all cases it must be conclusive, and give the impression of finality.

Characterization.—Later, as students of acting, we shall attempt to represent characters through the medium of our own personalities. Now it will be worthwhile to estimate the author's power of character delineation.

The playwright cannot take time to develop characters as the novelist does. He must project them, and allow them to reveal themselves through speech and actions. The one obligation the dramatist owes his audience is that his characters be consistent with themselves, and with human nature. If a vacillating weakling rises to the occasion, and meets a crisis like a hero, we should earlier have been given an inkling of his latent power. Otherwise he is not consistent with himself. One of Shakespeare's greatest attributes is his power of achieving unity of impression, through changes in time, place, and action, and unity in characterization. His people are always true to themselves in every situation. Their actions are unerringly consistent with human nature.

Any good play is well motivated. It is worth the student's while to examine the motives that actuate the characters in good fiction. As an actor, he must first understand these springs of action, and then learn to respond to them naturally.

Every play has one or two characters that dominate the plot. These must have some vital personal qualities to make them worthy of the prominence thrust upon them. The great Elizabethans followed Aristotle's dictum that all leading characters in serious drama must have the distinction of noble birth. Shakespeare's heroes were kings, princes, and noblemen. Ours may be only heroic hoboes. Birth to us has become "the guinea stamp." The man is the gold for our dramatic purposes.

What Makes Comedy Funny?—Comedy and farce are sometimes laughable and sometimes not. If they are not, they are listed as failures. This raises the question, What is funny?

Gustav Freitag may not have been altogether right in his analysis of humor, but it is worth while to examine his theory, which goes somewhat as follows: A man thinks he is sitting down into a chair and sits down on the floor instead. To those of us who are sufficiently primitive in our reactions—and who is not?—this accident is funny. It is a case of the man's expecting one thing and getting something shockingly different.

Now, there may be any one of three reasons for his sitting down beside the point. He might have himself miscalculated the position of his chair, which would make it his own fault—a lack of coordination, absentmindedness. This type of situation would naturally yield the comedy of character.

Again, the chair may have been too weak to hold his bulk and given way under him. In this case circumstances beyond his control are responsible, and we get the comedy of plot, or farce. Events conspire to make our hero ridiculous.

In the third place, someone may have pulled the chair away when he was not looking. In a play such a practical joker becomes the arch-intriguer, and we get the comedy of intrigue.

This theory of humor does not answer all the questions. Disappointed expectation is, no doubt, one prolific source of the laughable. But there must be a feeling of superiority on our part before we can laugh. Just today I saw two boys walking over a slippery place on the sidewalk. One of them slipped and fell, and the other burst out into the most hearty ha-ha's I have ever heard. In a moment he was down and the laughter ceased. We are inclined to laugh at those who fall only so long as we remain on our feet.

The comic element of character grows out of imperfections of character. Once upon a time physical injuries, bodily deformities, and even mental disorders were objects of mirth, both on and off the stage. To our civilized instincts these are anything but funny. Some of us may still laugh at the antics of a drunken man, particularly a stage drunk, because we expect him to act like a man and he doesn't. We enjoy laughing at remediable imperfections in character. The insane and the drunk act much alike. We may grieve at the first and laugh at the second, simply because the condition of the first is serious, while the condition of the second is temporary. In one case our feeling of superiority sobers us; in the other case it makes us laugh.

ASSIGNMENTS

Read a "well-made" play like *A Doll's House* and compare it with one of more liberal technique like *The Green Pastures*.

Read several plays under each of the following types:

Tragedy:
 Othello
 Hedda Gabler
 Mourning Becomes Electra
 Tragedy of Nan

Comedy:
 You Never Can Tell
 The Vinegar Tree
 The Silver Cord
 Candida

Melodrama:
 The Devil's Disciple
 The Green Goddess
 The Trial of Mary Dugan
 The Post Road

Farce:
 Importance of Being Ernest
 Ralph Roister Doister
 Man Who Married a Dumb Wife
 Nothing But the Truth

Read with careful attention to technique:
 Lady Windemere's Fan, Oscar Wilde
 The Second Mrs. Tanqueray, Arthur Wing Pinero
 Mrs. Dane's Defense, Henry Arthur Jones
 The Green Goddess, William Archer.

In *The Green Goddess*, the five steps discussed are very clearly outlined. Notice how the author utilizes the most modern devices, and how he locates his play to get the most unusual and colorful background. Note how fast events crowd upon the heels of the motivating force, how in one spot the action is seriously slowed by a long drawn out love affair of secondary importance, and how perfectly plausible is the unexpected resolution at the end.

TOPICS FOR DISCUSSION AND REVIEW

1. Discuss Freitag's logical Divisions of the play.
2. Review in outline the Exposition of one of the plays you have read, one that strikes you as rather cleverly managed.
3. To what extent may a playwright attempt to develop character within the compass of a play? What is his chief concern in presenting characters?
4. Discuss motivation as applied to drama.
5. What explanation would you give of humor?
6. What are the chief characteristics of melodrama? Of Comedy? Tragedy? Farce?
7. Name the motivating force in one of the plays you have read.
8. If only one set is used for a play, is there any reason for dividing it into acts?
9. How can you tell when the play has reached its climax?
10. Show how Clayton Hamilton's definition of a play divides the process of play production into its component parts.
11. How does the nature of the stage affect the technique of the play?
12. Why are many of the most popular plays destined for early oblivion?
13. What influence, if any, have the movies had on play technique?
14. To what source do present day dramatists like to go for their material?

CHAPTER II

ORGANIZATION

The first dramatic activity in England was carried on through amateur organizations, schools, churches, and trade guilds. In these groups drama had its inception, and, from them, it grew into an art of first importance, and a business of vast proportions. Ever since, there have been school dramatic organizations of one type or another. Often these have been frowned upon, and even suppressed, by a survival of that Puritan spirit which closed the London theatres in 1642. No further back than 1907, a young man applied for a position in a well known college in the middle west. He was asked to define his attitude toward the stage. When he admitted that he regarded the theatre as an important cultural influence, he was told his presence on the campus would be embarrassing. Student interest in the theatre was fought as desperately on that campus as any major vice would be today. But something happened during the following decade or two, for that college now supports a full-fledged dramatic department, with a fully equipped workshop.

Today our educators are taking dramatics seriously. More, and better, school plays are now produced annually in the United States than ever before.

Not so long ago, college dramatics were in the hands of students. Such organizations were student-controlled and student-directed. Students selected their own plays, and engaged their own coaches, who were, for the most part, unemployed actors with no notion of pedagogy, and little practical knowledge of play production.

As these organizations were not controlled, they often multiplied on a campus to such an extent that they interfered with one another, and with scholarship. To meet this condition, a member of the Faculty was appointed to regulate the activity, and soon the title of Director was applied to the person in charge of campus dramatics. This title, from the beginning, implied certain qualifications for the job, but today it is given only to specialists in play production. Under this new leadership, rival clubs were either merged into one, or entirely abolished. The Director was given charge of the reorganized group, or was permitted to organize the work as a departmental activity.

In various ways, play production in colleges and universities was placed on a sound academic footing. Several of our larger universities have endowed schools of the theatre. Many schools have completely equipped theatres of their own. In a large majority, the work is done through student organizations under the direction of experts.

A Typical Organization.—There is an infinite number of different types of student organizations, but the particular type does not matter, so long as it is suited to the conditions of the community. Since many high school groups constantly write for suggestions on organization, it may be well to outline a type that may serve as a working model.

First of all, an interesting, stimulating *name* should be selected. Finding this may be made into a

profitable game. A prize for the best suggestion may
be good advance advertising.

Then there should be a worthy *objective*. An article in the constitution of one dramatic group reads:
"To promote the cause of good drama in school and
community by the study, composition, and the stag-
ing of good plays, and by intelligent discussion of
the arts of the theatre."

At the head of the organization is to be the Director. Preferably, he would be a member of the
Faculty in full academic standing. Naturally, in a
student organization, he would be the only officer
not subject to student election. Other officers, elected
annually by students from among the members of
the group, would be the usual parliamentary officers, whose terms and duties would be described
in the constitution. These, together with the Director, and any number of elective representatives,
might constitute the Executive Committee. In a
large group, it may be advisable to delegate to this
committee full power to act in matters of policy
and business. In smaller groups, business may easily
be transacted in general sessions.

There may be as many grades, or degrees, of
membership as the local situation warrants.

Active members may be students in good standing, who have won membership through proven ability in acting, or proficiency in any of the stage arts.

Apprentices may be such students as offer themselves as candidates for the Active membership.
During their year or two of apprenticeship, they
would be assigned such tasks, and be subjected to
such tests, as the Director might devise to prove
their qualifications.

Associate members might be members of the Alumni, of the community, or of the Faculty, who can furnish the moral support, if nothing more.

Honorary members would be those who had earned admittance to national honorary dramatic fraternities. Such membership would be open to Active members as a reward for especially excellent work.

All rules and regulations adopted need to be very flexible, in order to allow easy adaptation to changing conditions. Given a trained Director, the type may be left to his discretion, but some form of organization is essential to progressive and permanent dramatic work in school or college.

The Staff.—Producing a play is a complicated task, with so many ramifications, that there is need for a careful division of labor among capable artists and workmen. These are usually called the producing staff. At the head is the Director. His co-workers would be the actors, the stage manager, the carpenter, the electrician, the prompter, the costumer, the property man, and the stage hands. Off the stage, the business manager, the box office attendant, treasurer, advertising agents, door man, and ushers work with him. The work may be still further subdivided, to enlist more students, but experience shows that a small, competent staff is more efficient.

The Director.—Although *director* is a comparatively new name in the theatre, it connotes a heavy responsibility, and a corresponding great opportunity. Play-directing in high schools is, at present, the most promising field for the university student interested in dramatics. In this connection, some of the qualities a student should seek to develop in training for this field of activity should be mentioned.

A good Director is qualified to give intelligent direction to his designer, carpenter, painter, electrician, costumer, stage manager, and, most intimately of all, to his actors. Even the playwright may often profit by his advice. To enumerate some of his most obviously valuable traits, a Director should have:

A quick, observant eye, good taste, and sound judgment.

A knowledge of drama, of stage conventions, and of the artistic value of the plays he chooses to produce.

A capable interest in all phases of production, even though he may be proficient in only one or two.

A thorough knowledge of the psychology of motivation, and of the art of showing motive through speech and action.

An appreciation of the nature of dialogue; its rhetorical qualities, its character values, its intellectual and emotional content.

A fair acting ability in his own right, which will enable him to get better results from his actors.

An imagination powerful enough to enable him to set his stage in his mind's eye, and to visualize the action as he reads the play.

A willingness to sacrifice social pleasures for the sake of seeing a play grow.

The industry to prepare in advance of rehearsals, in order to be authoritative on one hand, and helpful on the other.

The patience to wait for the desired effects to evolve naturally, and the realization that young actors cannot be forced into responses before they are mentally and emotionally ready for them.

An appreciation of the theatre that banishes the fear of a precarious livelihood.

Minnie Maddern Fiske used to say that a good director is willing to take off his coat and roll up his sleeves. He is not squeamish about using brawn as well as brain. Any student, ambitious to become a director, must resign himself to hard work and long hours.

A good director has the sensitiveness of the artist, the tact of a diplomat, and the backbone of a general. A wide experience in leadership is not amiss.

He allows the cast as much fun at rehearsals as is consistent with good work, but must also know how to secure concentrated attention during the progress of a rehearsed scene. Relaxation between scenes, and concentration the rest of the time, are both excellent props to the morale of any cast.

A director may be helpful in building character in his students by demanding a valid excuse for every delinquency of actors and staff, but he guards against allowing his annoyance with one member to spoil his friendly attitude towards unoffending members. He talks with the habitual offender in private, and if no improvement is forthcoming, dismisses him from the cast. He should be sympathetic when the need arises, and courteous always.

The director should be permitted to select his own plays as well as actors. He should welcome suggestions, but should reserve the right to disregard them. As so much depends upon the play and the cast, and as the director is held responsible for the work done, the choice of the play, and suitable talent, should be entirely up to him. The director should control all rehearsals, in person, or through able assistants.

It is his duty to determine the meaning of the play, and to work for the proper interpretation. He studies the acts, analytically for the general idea and totality of effect, and then, minutely, for acting opportunities. He maps out, in advance, his scene, plot and stage business. He cancels parts in the text that are inappropriate for his particular purpose, and he modifies the author's specifications, for settings and business, to suit his own stage facilities. He takes care, however, not to do any violence to the spirit of the play.

The office of director is most exacting of time, nerve-force, patience, and peace of mind. But when experience has taught one how to relax mentally and physically while hard at work, how to remain serene through all annoyances, how to secure maximum results with the minimum of effort, one will find it the happiest of avocations, or vocations, as the case may be.

The Actors.—No wise or friendly teacher would advise a student to seek the stage as a career. A *very* wise teacher, however, might modify such negative advice by saying that if the student has a strong enough urge, he will choose a stage career in spite of advice, in which case he has a good chance of success.

Acting is a great art, but no mediocre actor should be encouraged. The professional stage has fallen on evil days. It holds out little promise for the ambitious youngster. The amateur stage is at best only a pleasant avocation, well worth a student's serious attention for reasons of personal development, but not yet capable of yielding a livelihood.

If a student has in mind a stage career, he might ask himself some such questions as the following:

Have I *intelligence* to grasp the meaning of the play as a whole, and the quality of each part separately?

Have I *imagination* to put myself completely into the situation created by the author?

Have I *sympathy* to feel for, and with, the people in the play?

Have I *freedom of body* to inhabit the stage with ease, grace, and distinction?

Have I a *voice* that can be heard at a distance, one that is capable of expressing shades of thought and feeling?

Have I a *personality* enriched by thoughtful living, varied experience, and wide reading?

Have I the *ambition* that will drive me to sacrifice pleasure, comfort, and leisure for the sake of art?

Have I the *endurance* that will keep me constantly at work, and enable me to withstand the physical and nervous strain of a stage career?

Have I the scholarly tastes that will lead me to learn all there is to know about the drama and the stage? Have I a deep, abiding love of drama, or am I attracted by the superficial glamor of the footlights?

Do I like poetry, which indicates an appreciation of beauty, and a sense of rhythm and music in speech?

Am I interested in language: syntax, vocabulary, pronunciation, rhetorical elements, etymology?

Have I dramatic instinct, the knack of doing the right thing, at the right time, in the right place, in the right way?

Can I charm the audience into identifying themselves with me in any situation?

In a course in play production a student can discover the answers to some of these questions. As he appears in school plays, he can measure himself by these suggestions. At the end of his college term, he should have a fair notion of his potential dramatic ability.

The best preparation for the stage is no longer the stage itself. Such training still helps, but it is not in itself sufficient. A solid foundation of general culture, and specific training, is now indispensable, on the stage as everywhere else.

Business Manager.—Many schools are still satisfied to produce one or two plays a year as a class exercise, to pay off a debt incurred, or to provide a class party. Such sporadic, short-sighted work cannot bring the best results. It affords no systematic training for dramatic activity, and cannot have great cultural value. The importance of a permanent, active student dramatic organization is unquestioned.

In such an organization, the Business Manager has a responsibility second to that of the Director. It is his duty to keep the producing group solvent. He must secure a paying audience. He may manage the publicity, or he may appoint a student from the Journalism Department to take entire charge. He may manage the sales campaign, or find an alert student in the Commerce Department to do it for him. If he is a member of the faculty, he may take the entire burden upon himself: secure the theatre, arrange for printing; advertise the play; sell seats; arrange for the box office and ushers; and look after the comfort of the patrons. If he is an appointive student manager, he may find that most of his transactions are subject to the director's endorsement. For some reason, business men prefer to have the guarantee of a higher authority than a student.

A college group usually has some advance plan of production. It may undertake to produce two, three, four, five, or six plays during the school year. Two plays are hardly enough to keep in the spirit of the game, and more than six are rarely compatible with the college schedule.

If a program of good plays is mapped out each year, the manager's task becomes less exacting. A definite schedule of interesting plays, well produced, establishes a clientele that automatically guarantees an audience.

The manager's chief responsibility is to induce enough people to see the play to insure the financial success of the production. In order to do this, he must *advertise*. How, when, and how much are important questions for him to answer in each separate case. Many an amateur group has been a financial failure, not because their manager failed to advertise enough, but because he advertised too expensively. A professional company may gain by lavish advertising, for every dollar spent on display may return with interest. This is rarely true of local talent performances. In most cases paid advertising does not bring enough more business to pay for itself. This is particularly true if the play is an unspectacular piece of dignified literature.

The best publicity for a college play is available through the news columns of the local press. A display ad in the newspaper is valuable only to keep the good will of the publishers.

Posters, preferably student-designed, are very effective, if displayed to advantage. Announcements

Wilfred Lawson as himself.

by good speakers at convocations, and meetings of various kinds, are excellent advertising. The best results are obtained from personal solicitation in ticket sales campaigns. The main thing is to "tell 'em." People like to be told over and over again, until they are convinced that the play is the most important event of the year. There is a kind of inertia in every community which needs to be overcome in some way. It is the manager's job to make these people remember that there is a great play being produced for their special benefit.

The great advantage of having a whole year's program announced in advance is that it allows the manager to stage a ticket sales campaign at the beginning of the season. A reduced price season ticket has an important appeal, and the aim is to sell enough season tickets to guarantee the expense of the entire schedule. The gate receipts for each particular play, then, will be clear gain. The season ticket campaign concentrates effort, and minimizes the annoyance to the public.

The manager should always maintain an adequate reserve fund as producing a play costs money. No one has any moral right to gamble on the possible chance of coming out even. Many an amateur, as well as professional, venture ends with royalties unpaid, and with local business men holding the empty sack. Moreover, a large reserve fund justifies a more ambitious program, which in turn works towards increasing the reserve. If a group is subsidized in any way by student activities fees, or by appropriations, all is well. If not, the manager must guard against piling up bills that cannot be paid.

The office of Business Manager affords a live student an excellent opportunity to exercise talent in finance, and to develop traits that may be valuable to him after college. He must learn to be reliable in all his dealings, businesslike in settling obligations, courteous and honest in all his relations. It is his duty to see that the ticket booth is presided over with efficiency, that there be no embarrassing mix-ups in reservations, and that the audience leaves satisfied and eager to come again. It is the manager who keeps the group functioning. His work pays the royalties, rents the theatre, equips the stage, and keeps the treasury solvent.

Ushers.—The ushers should be selected for their ability to make patrons feel welcome. They should be carefully instructed as to seating arrangements, should know when and how to present flowers, and should be courteous and helpful in looking after the comfort of the audience at all times.

Prompter.—The prompter should be at rehearsals early in the rehearsal schedule, and he should familiarize himself with the requirements of the play. His chief duty is to see that all cues are promptly taken: light cues, curtain cues, music cues, entrance cues. He should see that all off-stage sounds are on time. He is of great value to the director during rehearsals, but the actors should not rely on him to give them forgotten lines. They should have done their job of memorizing too well for this.

Stage Manager.—The stage manager has charge of the entire stage crew. He supervises the work of the *grips* in setting up the scenes, and reviews the work of the property man to make sure everything is in place. He takes care that the electrician is properly instructed, and in short, is the director's handy man. If he is very efficient, he may relieve the director of the whole back stage responsibility and allow him to watch effects from the front.

The other members of the producing staff, designer, carpenter, painter, electrician and costumer, are important enough to deserve a chapter each. These mechanical phases will be treated in the second part of the text.

ASSIGNMENTS

Outline a model dramatic organization for the high school from which you were graduated, or in which you are a student. Give it an appropriate name, and define a worthy objective.

Study your classmates. Note their most obvious aptitudes. Then suggest which would do the best work as directors, actors, managers, etc.

Fix in your mind the following diagram:

ORGANIZATION

The Play

The Director

On the Stage	*Parliamentary*	*Off the Stage*
Stage Manager	President	Business Manager
Actors	Vice President	Box Office
Prompter	Secretary	Publicity
Make-up	Treasurer	Door Man
Wardrobe		Ushers
Properties		
Carpenter		
Painter		
Lighting		
Stage Crew		

TOPICS FOR DISCUSSION

1. Justify, or refute, the statement that organization is necessary for good work by school or amateur players.
2. If you were to take charge of a high school group, how would you begin?
3. Outline the duties of the Director in a school or college theatre.

4. What qualifications would you expect of him?
5. Would you advise any student to seek a stage career?
6. Outline the personal pre-requisites to success on the stage.
7. Suggest some new method of advertising a performance.
8. Why is a prompter needed?
9. In what way can you use what other departments in school to assist in dramatics?
10. Prepare a five minute statement of your ideas on the school or college theatre.

CHAPTER III

FINDING THE PLAY

The Director is responsible to his students, school, and community for the plays he produces. His own tastes and inclinations cannot always govern his choice, if he wishes to retain the good will and confidence of his patrons. To choose his program wisely, and with ease, the director should have a thorough knowledge of drama, and particularly of plays available to amateurs. He should take every opportunity to read new plays as they are published, and to see them as they are produced. If his acquaintance with the plays of all ages, and of all nations, is unlimited, his selections will show discrimination.

Unfortunately, the only produced plays most of us can study today are screen versions of current Broadway successes. These are sometimes very faithful transcriptions, but more often they violate the spirit of the original stage version. Any good director, who had to base his judgment of Sidney Howard's adaptation, *The Late Christopher Bean*, on Miss Marie Dressler's performance of it in the *talkies*, was sure to misjudge its excellent qualifications for the amateur stage. Many movie producers seem to be under the false impression that movie audiences demand horse play in their favorite entertainment. With that in mind, they made Miss Dressler do some outrageously inconsistent things, inconsistent with Abbie's character and with the obvious intention of the authors. Aurelia Rouverol's clever comedy, *It Never Rains,* sounded so inane and pointless on the screen, that no director, who had not read it in the original, would consider it a suitable vehicle for production as an amateur play. On the contrary, many comparatively trivial dramatic compositions have been glorified in the screen versions. The point is that a play written for the legitimate stage cannot be judged accurately by a screen production of it.

In selecting his season's bill, the Director considers several or all of the following problems.

1. *Authorship.* Some names are, in themselves, a guarantee of literary value. The few exceptions only prove the rule. A good name in the theatre is a more "immediate jewel" than a good name in man and woman, in Iago's maxim. Time-honored, and time-tested, plays are so numerous as to amount to an embarrassment of riches, and the Director who has a general idea of what is available is saved much time-consuming research. A number of usable plays of outstanding playwrights are listed under the assignments of this chapter. Most of them have been discovered, and tried out, by some ambitious producers, but there are undoubtedly countless others, equally good, still awaiting production.

There are many early plays without prominent authorship that may prove worthy of inclusion on any season's bill: *Gammer Gurton's Needle, Ralph Roister Doister, The Knight of the Burning Pestle.* Such plays are not only entertaining, but they hold an intrinsic historical interest.

Shakespeare should figure prominently in the plans of every college group. Perhaps few students are capable of sustaining the heights of one of the great tragedies, but the comedies and romances are quite within the scope of college students. In fact, when young people once realize how simple and spontaneous Shakespeare's language really is, in comparison with the stilted prose of many lesser dramatists, their enthusiasm rises. After all, Shakespeare's chief glory is his perennial youth, and his call to youth is irresistible when once understood. Even several of his contemporaries, Ben Jonson and others, may fit into a modern program occasionally.

The Restoration dramatists—Congreve, Farquhar, Vanbrugh, Wycherly—all have fair ratings as playwrights, but for a decidedly risque flavor, which might be suitable only as a very rare experiment.

Goldsmith and Sheridan are always acceptable, if their plays can be performed in the style of their period, both in costume and in the sense of comic values.

Lytton's sentimental, *The Lady of Lyons,* and mock-heroic *Richelieu,* would be interesting as examples of plays which once took the theatre-going world by storm, and held the stage long after their creator was forgotten. Robertson's *Caste, David Garrick,* and others, producible without royalty and in modern dress, are still dramatically dynamic.

Classic plays from France, Spain, Italy, Russia, and Germany, read in the classroom in the original, may be interestingly produced in translation, or in the original as an interesting experiment, if the necessary talent is available.

2. The *Audience.* Any community has the right to determine what is, and what is not acceptable in the entertainment field, as well as elsewhere. From the movies, and from professional road companies, they must take whatever is offered, and they take, without a qualm, plays that would make them

If I Were King, Act I, produced by The Dakota Playmakers.

squirm in their seats, if produced by local talent. It makes a difference whether their point of view is personal or impersonal. They do not worry much about their own morals, and they can stand offense to their own tastes, but they will not subject their offspring to the evil influence of a too, too sophisticated type of dialogue. The director of high school plays, particularly, must be careful not to worry the parents unnecessarily.

The greater the theatre-going experience of the community, the more freedom there will be in the choice of plays. The easily misunderstood, seemingly sacrilegious attitude of Mr. Shaw's *Androcles And The Lion* toward early Christian martyrs, for instance, would exclude it from most small communities. Even so harmless a play as *Another Language*, for general amateur use, must submit to all kinds of excision and modification of superlative expletives. The moral outlook of any community may be profitably broadened by a carefully graduated diet of good drama. Any severe shock is to be avoided, but a succession of minor quakes may be wholesome for all concerned.

3. *Stage Facilities*. The plays selected must not be too ambitious for the shape, size, and equipment of the local theatre. If the stage is small, with little back-stage space, plays in one setting are likely to be most successful. A small stage also suggests plays with small casts. The larger the stage, the larger the casts may be, and the more elaborate the settings. A spectacular melodrama, like *The Green Goddess*, is very nearly out of the question for a small stage. Possibly it could be done, but not according to specifications, and it would have to be so adapted as to spoil the play. For a large stage, with

sufficient back-stage room, nothing could be more appealing to the ambitious college group.

Many of the best plays do not need a stage at all for effective production. Shakespeare's *Midsummer Night's Dream, As You Like It,* and several others lend themselves to outdoor production, especially where the campus can boast a charming grove. Many plays can be produced without a setting on an artistically decorated platform. The knowledge of what to attempt under given conditions is more than half the battle.

4. *The Talent.* Before he selects his program for the year, the wise Director considers the problem of casting the plays. Before he decides to use *Hedda Gabler,* he makes sure that he has a Hedda among the women of his organization. Similarly, he must know where to put his hands on a Bill Jones before he undertakes the production of *Lightnin'.* If his available talent is limited, he cannot hope to do justice to a play like Pinero's *Thunderbolt,* in which the characters, seven men and six women call for experienced actors of genuine ability.

Much has been said pro and con on the subject of type casting. Whether he calls it type casting, or something else, the Director must look for, and find, an actor competent to carry the role assigned. In fact, it is quite the rule for a playwright to write his play with an actor or actress in mind. Edmond Rostand wrote *Chanticler* for Coquelin. Barrie wrote the *Little Minister* and several others for Maude Adams. Clyde Fitch wrote *Beau Brummel* for Richard Mansfield. This simply means that every great character creation calls for very definite mental, physical, and temperamental traits on the part of the artist who is to re-create this character on the stage. The Director must at least suspect the presence of these traits in one of his actors before he can confidently announce a play for production.

Then there is the question of age, and of experience. Members of the ordinary school and college group may range in age between fifteen and twenty-five. It is obvious that not many of these can grasp the middle-age point of view, and the mature implications of many great plays. The school director must fit his material to the mental and emotional age of his actors. Any primary grade may successfully undertake a play like *Alice In Wonderland*, but only people who have lived longer, and harder, can identify themselves with the characters in such plays as *The Master Builder*, or *The Wild Duck*.

5. *The Expense.* The school having its own theatre is fortunate. In such case a large part of the expense of production is eliminated. The money thus saved on theatre rental may be expended on more elaborate mounting.

Royalties are the next most worrisome item. While the royalty on some good plays may be nothing, on many—especially contemporary plays—it may amount to as much as one hundred dollars a performance. T. W. Robertson, Oscar Wilde, and Henrik Ibsen are among the best modern non-royalty possibilities. *Death Takes A Holiday* and *The Yellow Jacket* were originally held at one hundred dollars a night. Most first class English plays—Barrie, Shaw, Milne, Galsworthy—are keeping the royalty up to fifty dollars. As there is no moratorium on royalties, no director can afford to gamble on the prospective proceeds of a performance. He should have a comfortable reserve fund to work with. The larger this fund, the more expensive his selections may be. Where no nest egg exists, a good non-royalty play in an easy setting is indicated. A play like *A Doll's House* may be produced without much expense, and thus serve to establish a reserve for later, more expensive, productions.

Another item of expense is the costuming. Whether costumes are rented, purchased, or made, they are expensive. Plays like *Peer Gynt, Berkeley Square,* or *Snow White* must be shown in the proper dress, if the spirit of the play is to be strictly preserved. Many a play, old and new, requires dressing in the costumes of the nation in which it is set. In this case the expense of costuming may be materially reduced by an appeal to local residents of that nation for the loan of such garments of their native country as they may be treasuring as heirlooms. In a Scandinavian community, for example, a director would have little difficulty in borrowing the Hardanger peasant costumes appropriate for the production of *Peer Gynt.* Natives of Hungary might be happy to help out with the costuming of *Liliom,* and Checko-Slovakians would gladly assist in giving local color to *R. U. R.* In these ways a foreign play may be not only inexpensively dressed, but also effectively advertised.

6. *Variety.* To be attractive, a season's program must have as much variety as is consistent with other vital considerations. Life is not all tragedy— neither is it all comedy. It may even be enriched by a little nonsense now and then,—by melodramatic, farcical, or fantastic make-believe. An ideal dramatic season might offer a properly balanced diet of tragedy, comedy, melodrama, mystery, farce, and fantasy. Plays do not need to, and perhaps cannot, represent the same high level of excellence. A

simple, concentrated play like *The First Mrs. Fraser* may properly follow one of varied settings and grotesque costume and make-up like *Snow White And The Seven Dwarfs*.

Several nations may be represented in a season's bill. The American *Lightnin'*, the Norwegian *A Doll's House*, the Hungarian *The Guardsman*, and the English *Admirable Crichton* suggest a good variety in several respects. The preference given to any nation might depend upon the preponderance of any nationality in a given community.

7. *Purpose.* Finally, it makes a difference whether a play is intended for the purpose of entertainment alone, or for training apprentice actors. In some cases a director may be in position to run a double bill of plays. Those intended for the public would be selected with all of the aforementioned considerations in mind. Those chosen to give untrained actors the necessary experience or development would be limited only by their educational values. In the former case, the effect upon the audience is the sole concern; in the latter, it is the effect upon the student.

Many people still believe that it is better to give a good play poorly, than a poor play well. The fallacy is apparent. A play is not a play until it is produced, and a poorly produced play is a poor play, no matter how well it may have been written.

Students should undertake the very serious and tragic play with caution. Highly tragic emotions are apt to be outside the range of their experience, and, therefore, outside of their sphere of thought and feeling. Youngsters may get better training as well as better artistic results in sound comedy. They usually understand it better, and grasp its motivation more fully. This fuller perception will make for greater ease and spontaneity than they could possibly achieve in a play beyond their comprehension.

ASSIGNMENTS

The following partial list of classics that have been attempted by amateurs may serve to delimit the field for collateral reading:

SOPHOCLES: Antigone, Electra.

EURIPIDES: Medea, Orestes, Iphigenia, Electra.

ARISTOPHANES: Lysistrata (and others, naughty, but clever).

MOLIÈRE: Misanthrope, The Miser, Doctor in Spite of Himself.

BEAUMARCHAIS: Barber of Seville, Marriage of Figaro.

GOLDONI: La Locandiera.

LABICHE: The Voyage of Monsieur Perichon.

HAUPTMAN: Hannele, The Sunken Bell.

SUDERMANN: Magda, The Vale of Content.

BAHR: The Concert.

MAETERLINCK: Sister Beatrice, Monna Vanna, Death of Tintageles.

HEIJERMANS: Good Hope.

MOLNAR: Liliom, The Swan, The Guardsman, The Play's the Thing.

BENEVENTE: The Bonds of Interest.

SIERRA: The Cradle Song.

GIACOSA: As the Leaves.

PIRANDELLO: Right You Are, Six Characters.

IBSEN: Pretenders, Brand, Peer Gynt, Young Men's League, Pillars of Society, A Doll's House, An Enemy of the People, The Wild Duck, Hedda Gabler, Little Eyolf, The Master Builder, John Gabriel Borkman, Rosmersholm.

GORKI: The Lower Depths.

ANDREYEV: He Who Gets Slapped.

CHEKOV: Cherry Orchard, Sea Gull.

ARCHER: The Green Goddess.

BARKER: The Madras House, The Voysey Inheritance.

BARRIE: The Little Minister, Quality Street, The Admirable Crichton, Peter Pan, Alice-Sit-By-the-Fire, What Every Woman Knows, Dear Brutus, A Kiss for Cinderella, The Professor's Love Story, Mary Rose.

DRINKWATER: Abraham Lincoln, Bird in Hand.

GALSWORTHY: The Silver Box, Justice, The Pigeon, The Fugitive, The Skin Game, Loyalties, Old English.

HOUGHTON: Hindle Wakes.

MASEFIELD: Tragedy of Man.

HANKIN: The Cassilis Engagement.

JONES: The Silver King, Mrs. Dane's Defense, Mary Goes First.

MAUGHAM: The Circle, Our Betters, Lady Frederick.

MILNE: Belinda, Mr. Pim Passes By, The Dover Road, The Ivory Door, The Fourth Wall, The Truth About Blaydes.

PINERO: Sweet Lavender, The Magistrate, The Thunderbolt, The Second Mrs. Tanqueray, Trelawney of the Wells, The Amazons.

SHAW: Arms and the Man, Candida, You Never Can Tell, The Devil's Disciple.

WILDE: Importance of Being Earnest, Lady Windermere's Fan, The Ideal Husband, A Woman of No Importance.

ERVINE: The First Mrs. Fraser, John Ferguson, Jane Clegg.

O'CASEY: Juno and the Paycock, Within the Gates, The Silver Tassie.

EARLY AMERICAN PLAYS

BOUCICAULT: Coleen Bawn, The Shaughraun, Streets O' London.

MOWATT: Fashion.

HERNE: Shore Acres, Sag Harbor.

HOWARD: Saratoga, The Henrietta, Shenandoah.

THOMAS: Alabama, The Witching Hour, Arizona, Earl of Pawtucket.

GILLETTE: Held by the Enemy, Secret Service, Too Much Johnson.

THOMPSON: The Old Homestead.

MACKAYE: Hazel Kirke.

BELASCO: Girl of the Golden West, Return of Peter
     Grimm.
FITCH: Beau Brummel, The Climbers, The Truth, The
     Girl with the Green Eyes.
MOODY: The Great Divide.
KENNEDY: The Servant in the House.

In becoming acquainted with the plays here listed, the
student is certain to stumble upon others of equal importance. He may even uncover unsuspected possibilities
in new-old plays.

If you are studying drama in other courses, make note
of them for production purposes.

From among the plays you know, select six for one
season's program, carefully observing the limitations discussed in this chapter.

During the semester, as you have time, read the following, commenting on their suitability to your community:

> Berkeley Square
> Death Takes a Holiday
> The First Mrs. Fraser
> Outward Bound
> The Green Goddess
> R. U. R.
> The Beggar On Horseback
> The Cherry Orchard
> Liliom
> The Admirable Crichton.

Study several one-act plays for comparison of effects.

TOPICS FOR DISCUSSION

1. How far should the Director be responsible for the
   program of an amateur producing group?
2. Name four plays you would like to see produced this
   season, and justify your choice.
3. How does the moral outlook of a given community
   limit a Director's choice of plays?
4. What other important considerations enter into the
   planning of a season's program?

5. Would you ever attempt to produce a period play in modern dress?
6. Do you know of any good non-royalty plays, of another day, that can be produced without period costuming?
7. Would you select your plays first, and then find suitable actors, or know your available talent before planning your bill?
8. When is a play a good play?
9. Is the farce worthy of inclusion in a school program?
10. Would a serious play be preferable?

CHAPTER IV

FINDING THE ACTORS

Robin Starveling, you must play Thisbe's mother; Tom Snout
the tinker, you Pyramus' father; myself, Thisbe's father; Snug the
joiner, you, the lion's part;—and, I hope, here is a play fitted.
Shakespeare—*Midsummer Night's Dream.*

Having selected his play, or plays, for the season,
the director's next most important task is to choose
his cast. If there is an organization, for which ap-
plicants are tested in a series of tryout plays, the
director acting as judge, he already has a fair notion of the variety of talent he has to draw upon.
Indeed, as has been previously hinted, this knowledge probably has influenced his choice of plays.

What was said in a preceding chapter concerning
type casting will bear repeating. This system has
been openly deplored by many who were silently
approving it in their practice. They know that,
given a great role, the logical step is to find an
artist capable of interpreting it; or, given a great
artist, the most reasonable course is to find a great
role adapted to his peculiar gifts. Many an inferior
play has been glorified because the characters were
well fitted, and many a better play has failed because the star, carrying the brunt of the responsibility, was unsuited to the part.

The director may work the puzzle either way:
choose the play and find actors to fit; or know his
actors in advance and choose a suitable play. A
perfect actor would be capable of doing any imagin-
able role perfectly. It goes without saying that there

are no perfect actors. The star system is all wrong when carried to the extreme, as in some repertory companies. According to a rigid union code, when a manager engages a leading lady, she must retain that status while with the company, whether suited to a given role or not. In many cases, an exchange between the lead and the second might be better for the whole enterprise. But a contract is a contract, and this rule cannot be broken for any reason known to the profession.

The Moscow Art Theatre Group achieved unprecedented success, here and everywhere, because their star system was based on the requirements of artistic fitness, rather than on stipulations of a business contract.

Casting to type is justifiable, even from the pedagogic point of view. One objection has been that it fails to take a student sufficiently out of his everyday emotions and environment to have any broadening effect. This may be true, but the spontaneity he may achieve, in a role suited to his general make-up, compensates for any deficiency in breadth of experience. Casting in this fashion is educationally sound. It meets the student on his own ground, and there is no attempt to force him into a mould for which he is not prepared. The chief consideration, however, is that casting to type is necessary for the success of an amateur public performance. No wise director will jeopardize his chances of success, or pleasing his audience, by choosing his actors on any basis but that of fitness.

Just what does the term *fitness* imply? It does not mean that a boy should be cast for the role of a villain simply because he manifests unattractive traits in his daily life. It does not mean that a girl, simply because she talks baby-talk naturally, should be cast for a certain role in Booth Tarkington's *Seventeen*. Such casting would be unintelligent. There must be a more vital *correspondence* between role and actor. Let us consider some of the elements of this correspondence.

1. **Physical Fitness.**—*Weight*.—There are roles which cry for fat actors. Sir Toby Belch and Sir John Falstaff demand pronounced periphery, and unless a thin actor's cheeks are to be bulged out with putty, and his girth increased with pillows, the director must have a fat man available before he produces *Twelfth Night*, or *The Merry Wives of Windsor*. Sir Andrew Aguecheek, on the other hand, calls for a thin actor for two reasons. His lines are those of a very spindly man, and he is a comical foil for his corpulent companion.

Height.—Rosalind in *As You Like It* must be "more than common tall." This makes her taller than her constant companion, Celia. Often a playwright works the physical proportions into his dialogue, and actors with these qualifications must be found, or the lines changed. A good playwright understands the value of variety in height as in everything else. The lover is to be taller than his lass, unless the aim is comedy. Two or three characters, together frequently on the stage, should show as much variety in height as the *Three Musqueteers*, unless they are to represent twins or triplets. In such case, the variety would need to appear in some other phase.

The man is normally taller than the woman, even in actual life. On the stage, a short John and tall Annie would have a hard time radiating romance in a passionate love scene.

A tall actress is somewhat handicapped unless she can find a taller actor to match her on a scene. She must be satisfied to play some good unpaired matron, or dowager parts, a lone widow, or an odd old maid—parts by no means to be despised from the artist's point of view. A short man is out of luck for the same psychological reason. He must be willing to play character parts or comedy. It was the disappointment of the late Senator Robert La-Follette's life that he was too short to play *Hamlet*. There was a time, in the good old days of Kean, when acting was a matter of the spirit and intellect, when sheer artistry could make an audience lose sight of inappropriate stature. Those days are gone, and we like our heroes to look the part.

Complexion.—Many roles are actually motivated by color. Gentlemen prefer blondes, but not all gentlemen. An attractive ensemble must show a pleasing variety in coloring. A consistent variety in color of eyes, hair, and clothing dresses up the stage picture as nothing else can. A tall dark man and a small light girl, all else being right, are an ideal couple for stage purposes.

Voice.—That the candidate's voice must be strong enough to be heard in all parts of the auditorium is essential. The natural quality of the voice is equally important. Some voices are better able to express sympathy and tenderness; others, cold logic and irony. Suppose a cast is to be chosen for Wilde's *An Ideal Husband.* The most experienced and talented young lady in the organization might be the logical choice for the lead, *Lady Chiltern.* She has the necessary physical qualifications, but her voice has a persistent quality that would do scant justice to the part. It is not capable of expressing

Courtesy, Theatre Guild.

From *Porgy and Bess.*

the deeper, softer emotions. She can carry an important role, so what is to be done with her? There is an excellent ironic role in this play, that of *Lady Markby*. The candidate's voice is perfectly attuned to Lady Markby's hardened attitude toward life. The director has a choice of giving this young woman the part of Lady Chiltern, because she deserves the lead, or of casting her for Lady Markby, because she is vocally fitted to express the flavor of the ironic role. The former course would be a grave injustice to the actress, to the play, and to the audience.

2. **Mental Fitness.**—Clear thinking is a principal prerequisite to good acting. The power of clear, consecutive thinking, coupled with a vivid imagination is largely the basis of the actor's appeal to the audience. The candidate may have all the physical attributes indicated for the role, and yet lack dramatic intelligence. The actor must comprehend the role in all its bearings, and must understand the grammar and rhetoric of dialogue. He must be able to sense the literary quality of the composition to give it the intended meaning. He must be socially intelligent enough to enter fully into the life represented in the play. He ought to be clever enough not to betray confusion if any one in the cast should forget or miss part of the lines.

3. **Temperamental Fitness.**—The physically suited, intelligent candidate must also be analyzed for temperament. There are as many kinds of people in a play as there are in a similar group in real life. There are the quick, nervous, volatile types trying to play the game with the calm, stolid, phlegmatic folk. A calm, perfectly poised personality that would exactly fit the role of *Manson* in *The Servant In The House*, would not so easily fall into tune

with that of *Robert* in the same play. A practically minded young lady fitted to play the mother in *You Never Can Tell,* would not be very convincing as *Grazia* in *Death Takes A Holiday.* There is a kind of spiritual flavor which pervades every part in a good play, and a corresponding essence emanates from the personality best fitted to represent it.

If the director does not know his actors in advance, through a system of general tryouts, or through class-room association, he must institute a series of tests for those competing for parts. Among these tests may be any or all of the following:

1. *A reading test*—to show ability to grasp the logic and content of dialogue, and the vocal response to intellectual and emotional meanings.

2. *The pantomime test*—to discover co-ordination between mind and body, and reveal the candidate's power to express imagination and feeling through bodily movements.

3. *The voice test*—to evaluate the carrying power of the voice, clearness of articulation, and ease and expressiveness in modulation.

4. *The conversation test*—to show the applicant's force, ease, simplicity, and spontaneity in handling dialogue.

5. *The personal interview*—to bring out the characteristics not disclosed in other tests. David Belasco often chose his actors by inviting them to rehearsals, and by there observing their personal reactions to the episodes being rehearsed. The born actor is like a born race-horse: he cannot help showing his true mettle when face to face with a chance to act.

6. *The combination test*—to summarize the results of all the tests. The director should have a fairly reliable index of the diction, bearing, poise,

volubility, freedom from self consciousness, satirical feeling, and many other minor qualities.

Having tentatively chosen his players the director now completes the process of casting by satisfying himself on:

1. The candidate's conception of the role, sympathy with it, and grasp of the meaning of the play as a whole. Young actors, who have not studied Shakespeare enough to understand the rich associations of his thought processes, and the clear simplicity of his iambic pentameter style, invariably find the first two or three readings of one of his plays difficult. After working for some time under competent direction, they begin to see the excellent opportunities for genuine acting. The same may be true, in a lesser degree, of any play in its appeal to novices.

2. The candidate's probable contribution to the financial success of the play, or his local drawing power. No director will be so commercial as to sacrifice artistic to business success, but other things being equal, the candidate's wide acquaintance is a legitimate consideration.

3. The candidate's experience in leadership in school, church, or civic affairs proves a quality of character that effectively translates itself onto the stage.

4. Loyalty and length of service are to be recognized. A student who has been active in a dramatic group for three or four years, if he has always shown interest and ability, should be given precedence over a first year member, no matter how talented the newcomer may be. This serves the double purpose of rewarding merit, and keeping the tyro's head from getting too large for his old hat.

5. Congeniality is another vital consideration.

No matter how capable the candidate, if he cannot work in harmony with the rest of the cast, he is automatically disqualified.

6. Willingness to do any part assigned should carry with it its own reward. Those who immediately insist on the lead should be watched with suspicion. They are liable to be primarily interested in exploiting their own alleged ability.

7. The picture in its entirety should be considered in making the final adjustments in the cast. It is well to give careful thought to the ensemble, with balanced pictorial effects and physical and temperamental contrasts.

Casting the play is the director's highest prerogative, and his most delicate task. If he is not, for some reason, permitted to select his own actors, he should refuse to be called director. If one committee selects the plays, and another the players, the director has no legitimate function.

A wisely chosen play reading committee may be of value to the director, if it acts in a purely advisory capacity. A play casting committee may also be helpful in supplying data concerning the candidates. But, in order to be efficient, the director must be free.

It is understood that the director has learned:
To choose his actors fairly and intelligently.
"To play no favorites and let no favorites play him."
To guard against overlooking good talent.
To let ability outweigh suitability, where the two do not coincide.

A good director knows further:
That the most difficult middle-age parts are the most difficult for young people to play. Youth is their own province, and old age is not too exacting

with the aid of broad make-up. Perhaps they can also better appreciate the second childhood of age than the prime of life.

That a girl need not be pretty to be effective on the stage. However, the heroine, who is to be passionately loved by the hero, must be charming enough to earn the sincere admiration of the audience.

That a good stage personality is a mysterious element—something to be felt, rather than analyzed or explained.

That the surest test of an actor's general ability is whether he does the right thing, at the right time, in the right way.

ASSIGNMENTS

Select any of the plays you have previously read, and study the requirements of the various roles. Learn all you can about the special aptitudes of the members of your class, or group, and from among these select a tentative cast.

TOPICS FOR DISCUSSION

1. Present the plan you would use in casting a high school play, if you were the director.
2. Explain what is meant by casting to type. Would you care to justify it?
3. How should a candidate's qualifications for a given role be gauged?
4. Explain the effect of contracts on the stage.
5. What would be the probable effect of casting a tall girl and a short man for Juliet and Romeo?
6. Would you announce a play for production without knowing what talent there might be in your school?
7. How would you locate this talent?
8. What is your idea of a good stage personality?
9. What can the pantomime test reveal?
10. How much importance would you attach to a candidate's "drawing power"?

CHAPTER V

PREPARING FOR REHEARSALS

Before he calls his first rehearsal, the director has a clear conception of the spirit and meaning of the play to be produced, is thoroughly acquainted with all the characters, and has a clear impression of the motives that prompt their behavior. He has visualized the play so vividly that he has seen it produced—on the stage of his imagination. He has carefully gone through the text, omitting lines, and modifying such expressions as might be too strong for the taste of his prospective audience, and, where necessary, abridging very long speeches.

Many excellent plays, particularly those of the leisurely past, are too verbose. Ibsen's *The Pillars Of Society*, although intensely dramatic in its main line of development, is unfit for the temper of the modern audience due to the interminable philosophizing, in one or two acts. These parts may have been effective in the author's day when the philosophy was new and controversial. As it is now generally understood and accepted, a bare statement can convey the same idea without impairing the sense and purpose of the play. Long, involved speeches may still be effective when spoken by a great actor, whose personality and art are more interesting than his lines. The student actor, however, must let the drama carry the burden.

By reducing long speeches to essentials, the director not only reduces the play to more acceptable

61

time limits, but also saves it from a welter of barren speech-making. Properly edited, *The Pillars Of Society,* and several other older plays, are extremely effective on the stage. In their entirety, they would exhaust most theatre audiences. Oscar Wilde's plays, too, have been found to act better when subjected to this treatment.

In this process of cutting down, the director must be careful to do no violence to the spirit of the play, and to retain its intended meaning. Contemporary playwrights, thoroughly in tune with the mind of contemporary audiences, do not need any cutting down, as they have reduced the conversation to the lowest terms. On the other hand, they may need considerable revision. What is written for a sophisticated public must be adapted for a more easily shocked amateur public. The author, if he were writing specifically for the latter, would modify his language to suit their taste, and not many playwrights would object to an occasional change in their scripts.

The director's next step is to study the stage directions given in the text for consistency, and with his local stage facilities in mind. He also marks any necessary revision in the margin of his prompt book.

Stage directions given in copies of old plays are based on the obsolete wing and groove system of stage setting, before the box set came into general use. There were two, three, or four wings pushed into the proscenium opening from the side and parallel to the back wall. The spaces between these wings were used for entrances. The character might enter through the first, second, or third opening on either side of the stage.

An excellent old farce, *The Obstinate Family,* gives directions as follows:

The reader is supposed to be on the stage, facing the audience. From this position L would mean left; R, right; S.E.L., second entrance left; S.E.R., second entrance right; U.E.L., upper entrance left; U.E.R., upper entrance right; C is center; L.C. left of center; R.C. right of center; T.E.L. and T.E.R. third entrance left and right respectively. L.C. and R.C. could mean either openings in the back wall, or positions of furniture on any section of the stage right or left of the imaginary line dividing the stage into right and left halves. Often these symbols were figures, as R.2E., or L.2E., meaning right second entrance, or left second entrance. Such directions must be entirely disregarded by the modern director, except as they may indicate to him the general positions of his doors and windows. In modern plays better results may often be achieved by disregarding the plan given in the text of the play.

Many playwrights have a keen sense of stage effects, and their prescribed business may safely be followed, while others lack this ability. Even with it, a playwright might be the first to advise revision after watching a rehearsal of his play. Frequently plays are printed as submitted by the author, *before* the directions had been tested out in actual production. When local stage facilities are inadequate, the director may design a picture for himself. This automatically cancels all stage business indicated in the text. It is then up to the director to devise stage directions to suit his own design. This mapping out of stage business in advance of rehearsals is the director's most important preliminary work. If he has done this well, his hardest job is finished. Satisfactory rehearsals are assured.

Producing a play is not the simple matter that it appears to the audience. The simpler it seems in its final effect, the more carefully the details of stage business have been worked out.

The stage has a very definite technique, variable in its surface manifestations, but based on a few fundamental principles. These are the skeleton which the director must conceal under a veneer or flesh and blood in speech and in action. If this skeleton protrudes too much at any point, the advance planning has not been done well.

A director usually works out his productions in some such way as this. On a stiff piece of paper he draws a large floor plan, sketching in doors, windows, and furniture, as indicated by the author of the play. With the ground plot before him, he lets chess men, thumb tacks, or other simple objects represent the characters in the scene. Those representing characters on the stage when the curtain rises he places in effective positions. From this point he moves his symbols from position to position as he reads the text. New objects are added to represent new entries as the scene progresses; the stationary and shifting positions are tested for their probable effect; and satisfactory results are noted in the margin of the prompt copy.

The director, whose imagination is strong enough to carry the details of the scene in his mind, may not need to resort to such objective aids. He sees as he reads, and he reads to remember. But most directors, particularly those less experienced, will find this ocular proof of the effectiveness of their stage business very helpful.

If I Were King, Act IV, produced by The Dakota Playmakers.

Satisfied that he knows his play thoroughly in every dimension, the director is now ready to call his first rehearsal. At the first meeting he reads the play through to the assembled cast, to impress upon their minds the effect of the whole play, and a clear picture of the people in it. To assure active attention, and relieve possible monotony, he may ask some of the cast to help out with the reading. He will discuss the play, and ask questions. On the basis of the answers he gets, he may decide to reassign the parts.

At the second meeting he may have the cast walk through the business mapped out in advance. To get the positions and movements properly fixed in the minds of the cast takes time and energy. Hence, it is rarely advisable to go through more than the first act at the second meeting.

At the third rehearsal the first act may be reviewed for the business, and another act may be worked out in detail.

At the fourth rehearsal the cast should be taken rapidly through the entire play, reading the parts and walking through the business. By this time the lines of the first act should be memorized. By the end of the second week of rehearsals the whole cast should be able to go through the entire play without the aid of their books.

A detailed discussion of Stage Business will be found in a succeeding chapter. Here we are taking up the director's method of preparation and rehearsal.

Among professional directors, three methods are in use:

1. *The laissez-faire method,* under which good actors are engaged, and are permitted to work out

their salvation without much intervention from the director. This would appeal to the indolent or careless teacher, or one who has no particular *vision* of the play he wishes to have realized in the production.

2. The *imitation method,* under which the director insists on having every detail of speech and action conform to his own ideas. This is naturally productive of inferior copies of the director's own individuality. This method is a favorite with coaches who go from place to place, organize, rehearse, and produce a play in two weeks, get their fees and depart, leaving no constructive experience behind.

3. The *combination method* permits, and encourages originality in the actors, the director assisting to bring out his idea of the meaning of the play, without destroying the personalities of the players. This is obviously the wisest of the three methods. It leaves the actor free to use his own ingenuity, and to preserve his own individuality, at the same time enabling the leader to weave the separate individualities into a well unified pattern of teamwork.

Adopting the combination method, the director may set up for his guidance some such maxims as follow:

I shall not try to cover too much ground at any one rehearsal, lest it prove confusing to the cast and lessen their enthusiasm for the play. Two or three hours of work at a stretch will be sufficient.

I shall impress upon all members of the cast that no time is to be wasted during rehearsals in learning lines. Psychologically speaking, a rehearsal may be the best place to learn lines, but it wastes too much time for all concerned.

I shall insist that each member of the cast study the lines of his co-partners on the stage, in order to follow the logic of the development more easily, and to get truer emotional responses.

I shall try to imagine each successive episode of the play so vividly myself, that my mental picture may communicate itself to my actors. If this does not happen, I shall take pains to explain as clearly as necessary.

I shall insist on good order and serious work during rehearsals, but with short intervals between scenes for relaxation and fun. Complete relaxation, following a period of intense concentration, is good discipline for any cast.

I shall accept cheerfully any valid excuse for tardiness or absence, but will permit no habitual delinquent to steal time from me, and other members of the cast, by spoiling the full value of the rehearsal.

I shall discourage any inclination toward direction of one member by another. Some amateurs develop this habit unconsciously to the great annoyance of others, and to the detriment of group morale.

I shall encourage each actor to invent as much interesting business as he can, and later eradicate what does not contribute to the desired effect.

As far as possible, I shall train my actors by *evolution* rather than by *revolution,* to arouse their latent abilities rather than supply them with a superficial veneer.

I shall not hesitate to alter preconceived plans whenever necessary. It often happens that amateurs find it impossible to express themselves effectively in one position on the stage, but do so quite readily in another. By trial-and-error methods, if necessary,

I shall work till I find the right combination for the troublesome scene.

I shall have all entrances and pieces of furniture in use clearly marked from the beginning, even though I cannot have my stage completely set before the final rehearsal.

I shall avoid making too many suggestions to the cast at any one time. As rehearsals progress many things will adjust themselves without my suggestion, and be all the more spontaneous for it.

I shall try to remember that no two people can be taught in exactly the same manner. One may need vigorous language, while another responds better to gentle admonition. With some a good job may even be made better by a word of praise.

I shall strive to preserve the actor's individuality at all cost to my patience and desire for quick results.

I shall avoid forcing my actors into responses before they are emotionally ready for them. Many things that are often worried over, and worked for, during the early rehearsals, later come easily at the slightest hint.

I shall refuse to show an actor how to read his lines, except as a last resort. I shall explain the sense and the motive for the line, and let him say it in his own way. This will be the right way, providing the actor has enough intelligence to be on the stage at all.

I shall not waste the precious moments of the rehearsal time by stopping to explain details of personal action and interpretation. Such problems will be worked out with individual actors in private session.

I shall not halt a rehearsal that is going well in

order to make minor corrections. I shall rather take notes and make my corrections at a convenient stopping point.

I shall work with properties as early as possible, and, with the assistance of a prompter, I may be free to move about as I am needed and to watch effects from a distance.

When the lines have been mastered and the scene is going smoothly, I shall begin to work for tempo, emphasis, suspense, and characterization. I shall use my voice as a musician uses his baton, throwing out such hints as: *faster, retard, hold, stronger, pause.*

I shall allow myself at least four weeks of daily rehearsals, or spread at least twenty-eight full rehearsals over a longer period.

I shall be cheerful always, especially at dress rehearsal and final performance. I shall be as easy and as confident as I wish my actors to be.

I shall ask small groups of visitors to be present at a few of the final rehearsals in order to put fresh zest into the work.

Finally, I shall remember that there is no such thing as too much rehearsal, unless it amounts to mental and physical fag. The more rehearsing there is, the smoother the performance is bound to be.

ASSIGNMENTS

Choose one of the plays you have read under previous assignments. Study the requirements of action, map out your business, and block out your rehearsals.

Choose members of your class for the characters in your play and let them read the parts, walking through your prescribed business.

The members of the class are expected to watch the performance, and to make constructive criticism.

CHAPTER VI

TRAINING THE ACTORS

VOICE AND LINE READING

Training the actor's voice may not be the province of the professional director, but should be among the many duties of the teacher-director. If the candidate's voice is not developed to its full possibilities, the director can make an effort to improve it. In a school or college course in Play Production, several weeks may be profitably spent in starting voices on the right road.

The importance of the voice in acting may be gathered from the following quotations from recognized authorities:

"Consider your voice: first, last, and always your voice."—*Mrs. Fiske.*

"Get control of your means, especially your voice."—*E. H. Sothern.*

"Learn to use your voice, not to abuse it."—*Richard Mansfield.*

"No matter how much we know about acting, we must depend upon our voices to express it. Tones are most important, and these can be cultivated. Indeed, they may be said to be the result of cultivation in most actors. Nature gave them the instrument, but she did not teach them to play it."—*Louis Calvert.*

Most writers on the subject analyze the voice into the elements of Time, Pitch, Force, and Quality, which are all to be found in the speaking or singing voice. They may be studied separately and then combined into an unconscious total effect. But for a more rapid development of the actor's voice, training may be simplified by emphasizing three elements:

I. Beauty
II. Flexibility
III. Power

These three phases come as near as any other to covering the entire ground, and they are mutually exclusive enough to furnish a method of effective drill.

Beauty involves purity and resonance—rich vibrancy in a wide range of pitch.

Flexibility takes in articulation, enunciation, inflection, and the effortless shifting of the voice from pitch to pitch, or modulation of tone, melody.

Power is a matter of muscular control. It resides partly in the inter-costal muscles, but principally in the diaphragm.

Strength and vitality of voice come from the diaphragm. New born babes instinctively use this muscle to draw in the breath of life. Adults too often lose the muscular sense in that region of the body, and can only regain it by a conscious effort. Too many voices are spoiled for singing and speaking by the bad habit of squeezing the breath out of the lungs laterally through collapsing the chest. This is bound to result in a shallow, breathy tone, and a voice of slight endurance. People have lived, spoken, and have even sung acceptably without having known the proper use of the diaphragm, but they might have lived longer, and been the better artists, had they learned to control this chief muscle of respiration.

No voice can be greatly benefited by text-book exercises, unless they are intelligently practiced under the direction of a good teacher. The following suggestions are representative of those in most books, on the voice, but every good teacher will find, and adapt, exercises to fit each particular problem.

The ideal voice would be the result of a column of completely vocalized air playing freely between the diaphragm at one end and the center of the lips at the other. Scientific placing of the voice is a matter of directing this current of air into the proper spot of a properly shaped mouth. This natural spot is the center of the lips, with the buccal cavity so broadened as to afford generous resonance area, and with the palate so trained as to allow tangents of the current to strike up through the nasal passages and set up vibrations in the resonance chambers of the head. The best voice comes from a relaxed, yet thoroughly vitalized, attitude of the whole body. A student of voice will do well to reflect upon the following statements:

Conceive a fine ideal of vocal strength and purity, hold it always before the mind's ear, and compare your own voice as you speak. As the lad who watched the *Great Stone Face* unconsciously grew to resemble it, so you may gradually approach your ideal in vocal quality.

Do not rest satisfied until every harsh click in the initial vowels, and all other impurities have been cleared up.

Keep adjusting and re-adjusting your articulative organs until you find the positions that yield the best results.

Cultivate, in your speaking voice, a decisive conversational edge. Avoid the monotone commonly heard in reading.

Hold the thought that *the voice naturally shapes itself around the image or object present in your mind*. It instinctively spreads itself out to do justice to the idea of the ocean or mountain, and just as instinctively shrinks to the proportion of a speck. Any natural story teller knows how to respond vocally to the GREAT BIG BEAR, the MIDDLE SIZED BEAR, and to the teeny weeny little bear. This psychological response of voice is sometimes called *vocal language*. Vocally we can make a mountain out of a molehill, or a sparkling brook out of the Amazon River, but the effect would be ludicrous.

The actor has a special problem in that he is not speaking directly to the audience, but intimately to his fellows on the stage. This does not mean that he neglects his audience vocally. He must speak directly to his colleagues, *but he must be conscious of a generous bulge of tone into the auditorium*.

EXERCISES

Beauty.—In order that there may be pure tone, the throat must be free and open. The root of the tongue, which often shows a tendency to rise like the back of an angry cat, must lie flat or slightly hollowed in a sort of trough along the bottom of the mouth. During a hearty yawn the tongue behaves exactly right for vocalization. Simulate a yawn, and note the *feel* of the positions the various parts of the mouth and throat take in the process. Try to retain that feeling while vocalizing. *The current of vocalized air must have an unobstructed right of way from the larynx to the lips.*

Exercise the soft palate until it automatically lifts itself out of the way to permit free passage of sound vibrations to the resonance chambers of the nose and head. Nasal quality is the result, not of forcing the breath through the nose, as commonly supposed, but of shutting the nasal passage off by habit or malformations.

Make humming, with or without musical accompaniment, a constant habit. When humming keep the lips lightly touching together, but open the teeth as wide as possible to form a large resonance area in the buccal cavity. Prolong musically the sound of *m*, then of *n*, and then of *ng*. Make these sounds separately at first, then change from one to the other in quick succession without interrupting the flow of tone: *m-n-ng, m-n-ng*.

Intone the following syllables, pushing the consonants strongly against the front walls of the mouth:

Mah, may, mee, mi, mo, moo.

Nah, nay, nee, ni, no, noo.

Start by striking each syllable separately, staccato; then speak them in a continuous stream of tone. Finally bend the stream of tone to various melodies. Commit to memory and practice verses rich in musical combinations:

"O, sing and wake the dawning,
O listen to the wind!
The night is long, the current strong,
My boat it floats behind."
—*Swinburne*.

"O moon in the night, I have seen you sailing,
And shining so round and low,
You were bright, ah bright, but your light is failing;
You're nothing now but a bow."—*Ingelow*.

Utter with force:
Ring, sing, swing.
Ringing, singing, swinging.
"Ring, grandpa, ring, oh ring for Liberty!"

Find, learn, and practice literary bits of resonance quality.

Flexibility.—Repeat slowly and carefully at first, more rapidly as you gain fluency, passages like the following, taking care to place the articulative organs in exact position for all consonant-vowel combinations, to finish the consonant of the preceding word before attacking the initial sound of the succeeding word, and to keep all tones as lightly as possible on the lips. The difficult combinations are italicized.

"Make up your mind *that you* will be heard, *that you* will be understood, and this determination will make you speak distinctly, enunciate clearly, so that the boy in the *last seat* of the gallery may hear without effort the *tiniest syllable*. Toss off the *t's* on the tip of the tongue; fling the *f's* off with a flip; burst the *b's* bubblingly; put the *p's* lightly on the lips; mingle the *m-n-ng's* musically; sound the vowels with a full tone, and your speech will be music in your mouth."

In the sounds of *f* and *v* the upper teeth rest firmly on the lower lip. With that in mind, practice:

"The foul fiend flibbertigibbet."
"Elaine the fair, Elaine the lovable. ."

The sound of *b* and *p* is made between the lips. Practice such combinations as:

"I bubble into eddying bays, I babble on the pebbles."

As if you were intensely interested in giving excellent vocal advice to your classmates, speak the following in a conversational, intimate, friendly manner:

"Speak the speech I pray you as I pronounced it to you—trippingly on the tongue. But if you mouth it, as many of our players do, I'd as lief the towncrier spake my lines. Do not saw the air too much with your hands, thus; but use all gently. For in the very torrent, tempest, and, as I may say, whirlwind of your passion, you must beget and acquire a temperance that will give all smoothness. O, it offends me to the soul to hear a robustious, peri-wig-pated fellow tear a passion to tatters, to very rags, to split the ears of the groundlings, who, for the most part, are incapable of anything but inexplicable dumb shows and noise. I'd have such a fellow whipped for o'er-doing Termageant. It out-Herods Herod. Pray you, avoid it."—*Shakespeare.*

Power.—Hold the chest up firmly, without tension. Keep the intercostal muscles flexibly alert. Expand about the waist in such a way as to draw air into your lungs. With the aid of the transversalis muscles of the abdomen, push up against the bottom of the lungs, forcing the breath out from below. This column of air, properly vocalized, should result in a strong, rich, vital tone.

Sit erect in a chair and practice breathing downward, pushing the abdomen out as you inhale. Then expel the breath easily by lifting the diaphragm up under the floating ribs. If you fail to get the proper muscular combination in the sitting posture, try lying flat on your back and practice breathing with the rise and fall of the abdomen. When you have succeeded in getting the *feel* of this, try it standing on your feet. Practice this method of breathing until it gets to be second nature.

Inhale downward, then expel the breath violently with one strong contraction of the diaphragm.

Count up to six with separate strokes of the diaphragm, then count to the same number with one steady contraction.

Practice all the exercises given under Beauty and Flexibility with special attention to muscular control.

Find stronger passages like the following:

"Again among the hills, the shaggy hills!
  The clear rousing air comes like a call of bugle notes
      across the pines,
  And thrills my heart as if a hero had just spoken.
    Again among the hills!
  The jubilant, unbroken, long dreaming of the hills!"
                    —*Richard Hovey.*

"Once more unto the breach, dear friends, once more,
  Or close the walls up with out English dead!
  In peace there is nothing so becomes a man
  As modest stillness and humility,
  But when the blast of war is in our ears,
  Then imitate the action of the tiger!"
                    —*Shakespeare.*

"Room, my Lords, room! The minister of France can need no intercession with the king!"—*Lytton.*

The Voice and Dialogue.—Every speech in a play has double *content*: intellectual and emotional. In like manner, every speech has its appropriate *form*, or method of conveying to others this double content. Dr. Woolbert disposed of the matter by suggesting that every speech has intellectual content and personal intent. The speaker tells not only what he *means*, but also how he *feels* about it.

The actor must form the habit of realizing the content before speaking the words that convey it. This is a matter of mental discipline. Some people acquire the habit in childhood, but others must achieve it in adult life by patient mental application. This habit is fundamental to all successful reading, acting, or speaking. Saying the words of a speech with "damning facility" is no part of intelligent acting. The content, and the intent, must instantly become a part of the actor's mental and emotional experience, if the form he gives it is to ring true.

The *form* may be an object of careful cultivation. It involves all the agents of expression, including the whole body. Fortunately, adequate realization of the content suggests the appropriate form of expression.

The actor of today must create the illusion of actual conversation, which is characterized by simplicity, spontaneity, and rich variety. These are even more important on the stage than on the platform. In the exercises given at the end of this chapter, some principles formulated out of the habits of conversation are suggested for practice. They do not pretend to cover the entire ground, but they should suffice to call attention to the more common difficulties encountered in making the line *read* sound like a bit of conversation *spoken*.

The emotional content is expressed through bodily response and vocal quality. Every emotion has its own language in *tone*. The stage lover, whose tones remain didactic or business-like, will never be suspected of being in love with the heroine. Cupid may have "clapped him on the shoulder" several times in real life, but on the stage the audience will "warrant him heart-whole."

In William Butler Yeats' *The Hour Glass*, the Wise Man's well-taught pupils come in at the end of the play to find their teacher's head resting on his arms across the table. In boisterous tones of cynicism and raillery, they tease the tired wiseacre, until one of them hap-

Set for *Smilin' Thru*, designed by a local stock company artist.

pens to touch his shoulder. He exclaims, "Oh, he is dead!!" The tone he uses sweeps away every vestige of the bantering atmosphere, and sends the sophisticated young men to their knees.

As has been said, modern acting has no place for the old style declamatory manner. Actors today more than ever before are expected to *talk*.

Students may profit by considering the implication, and the application of the following statements:

1. Read your line in *context*. In other words, keep your eye on what has gone before, and speak your speech in logical connection with what has been said in preceding speeches. In the second speech in the first Act of *As You Like It*, Old Adam says, "Yonder comes my master, your brother." It is an extremely simple speech and easy to pronounce. The normal melody is so obvious that nearly every student reading it for the first time, will read it in the normal stress: "Yonder comes my *master*, your *brother*." The trouble is that the reader sees it as a unit by itself, as if Orlando had not been talking at considerable length about this very brother. But because Orlando has already established his brother Oliver in the minds of the audience, the *context* makes the stress fall on *comes*. We are talking about Oliver, and there he *comes*. It is such undiscriminating lapses in the logic of dialogue that mark the untrained reader.

2. Fix your attention on the key word of your speech, and set it forth emphatically when you come to it with slide of voice, stress, inflection, and even gesture if need be. Key words in a sentence may be compared to stones across a brook. To carry the full force of meaning, these have to be aimed at, and landed on, vocally. Again, graceful speech behaves like a bird in flight. The wings give a few flutters and then sail, a few more flutters, and sail. In the same way the voice approaches the key words: an easy, rapid approach, and then the slide that carries meaning.

3. Base your line reading on your best conversational style. Later you may add character peculiarities.

4. A careful placing of emphasis marks the progress of thought in a scene; a varied tone quality indicates the ebb and flow of feeling.

5. In any scene between two or more speakers, one carries the burden. He naturally speaks in a more dominant tone than the others. He may talk and the other listen, or he may ask questions and the others answer. Such give-and-take may continue for an entire scene, or the burden may shift frequently according to the subject of the scene.

In the opening episode of Wilde's *A Woman of No Importance*, Lady Caroline leads off with a volley of questions, and she keeps her lead, while Hester and Sir John merely chime in quietly with their modest answers.

6. Each speech has its own appropriate tempo, and this should not be affected by the tempo, or momentum of the scene as a whole. A slow witted speaker would need to speak slowly, even though the farce may have a fast pace. Touchstone rattles away with fine facility, while Audrey and William drawl as lazily as they think.

7. In speaking any kind of memorized passage try to give the impression that it is being born in your mind at the moment of utterance. Show your mental processes as you speak. Realize the full content of your language before you give it voice.

8. Bodily and facial expression normally precedes vocal expression by a perceptible interval. Show the emotional effect of your thought through bodily response, *look* the thought through appropriate facial response, and then give it voice. These three acts will be almost simultaneous, in point of time.

9. A well-motivated *pause* may speak volumes in itself. It may grip the audience compellingly, where unbroken speech at the point would not register any effect at all. The pause is emotional, it suggests power, and it is always significant. To be effective it must be more than mere hesitation. It must have sound psychological grounds to rest upon. It must be filled with thought, feeling, or purpose. The unmotivated pause is sometimes necessary to avoid killing a laugh. Such unnatural break may be bridged over by continuing bodily and facial expression, which may serve to prolong and enhance the amusing situation.

10. Attention is largely controlled by a striking variety in vocal and bodily responses. A sudden change in

tempo, or in vocal quality, arrests attention more effectively than great stress at regular intervals.

To sum it all up, the best advice to give for reading lines is, *don't read them—talk them.*

Use common sense in reading. Imagine there is someone in the next room listening. See if you can deceive him into thinking that you are not reading, but talking to somebody in the room with you.

Be mentally on your toes all the time.

Use your most discriminating intelligence.

Keep your imagination alive.

Draw upon your experience of life, call upon your knowledge of human nature and give free play to your emotional powers.

Keep your articulative organs finely sensitive.

Make your tones, on final syllables of your sentences, firm and strong.

Form your vowels *largely*, for carrying power.

Practice, Practice, PRACTICE!

The amateur reader, in his subtle perversity, has many ways of deviating from the norm of natural conversation. The following principles are based on the habits of conversation. As they are also most frequently disregarded in vocal interpretation, the student actor may find it helpful to try some of them out in practice. They are all taken from familiar literature. In their statement they may seem superfluously obvious. In their application they are by no means generally observed.

Practice the quotations with the statement in mind. Find other examples of the same sentence forms.

1. A group of words naming a single idea are spoken closely together as so many syllables of the same word.

> "So still the air that I can hear
> *The slender clarion of the unseen midge.*"
> "*The huddling trample of a drove of sheep*
> Tilts the loose planks."
> *—Lowell.*

Notice that it takes *all* the words to name a single sound.

2. In a suspended sentence, the voice takes the rising inflection until the conclusive phrase is reached.

"Though yet of Hamlet, our dear brother's death
  The memory be green; and that it us befitted
  To bear our hearts in grief, and our whole kingdom
  To be contracted in one brow of woe,
  Yet so far hath discretion fought with nature
  That we with wiser sorrow think on him,
  Together with remembrance of ourselves."
                      —Shakespeare.

3. In a loose sentence the voice may fall at each comma which sets off an added phrase.

"And thus the land of Cameliard was waste, thick with
    wet woods,
 And many a beast therein, and few or none to scare or
    chase the beast."
                      —Tennyson.

4. In an extended simile, or comparison, all elements in the first part take the rising inflection, while all in the second part may take the falling inflection.

"But as the cur, plucked from the cur he fights with, ere his cause be cooled by fighting, follows, being named, his owner, but remembers all, and growls remembering; so Sir Kay beside the door muttered in scorn of Gareth whom he used to harry and hustle."—*Tennyson.*

5. Words and phrases in apposition take exactly the same vocal direction as the elements they modify.

"Then at his call, 'O daughters of the Dawn
  And servants of the Morning-star, approach,
  Arm me,' from out the silken curtain folds
  Barefooted and bare-headed three fair girls
  In gilt and rosy garments came:"
                      —Tennyson.

6. Elements in the inverted order take exactly the same stress and inflection as if they were in the normal order.

"*Sleeps* the brimming tide."—*Lowell.*

"*Hands,* large, fair, and fine."—*Tennyson.*

7. Verbs introducing quoted statements take the rising inflection without pause or stress.

> "And Gareth said,
> Full pardon, but I follow up the quest,
> Despite of Day and Night and Death and Hell."
> —*Tennyson.*

"To whom the mother said, 'True love, sweet son, had risked himself and climbed, and handed down the golden treasure to him.' "—*Tennyson.*

8. A question does not always mean a rising inflection; neither does the period always take the falling.

Compare: "Which one will you have?"
With: "Are you finishing college next spring?"
Compare: You may go now. I am through with you.
With: Don't go yet. Stay a little longer, friend.

9. Elliptical statements are spoken exactly as if the missing elements were present.

> "Sunset, and evening star,
> And one clear call for me."
> —*Tennyson.*

10. In each succeeding statement it is the *new* element that receives the stress and slide of voice.
"And thus the land of Cameliard was waste . . . , and
      many a *beast* therein,
And none or few to *scare* or *chase* the beast."
11. A connective, followed by a subordinate phrase, is grouped *with* the subordinate phrase. The comma must not affect the voice movement.
"And Gareth went, and, breaking into song, sprang up."
The point is that punctuation is for the eye, not for the voice. Don't let every comma trick you into a pause, nor every period into a falling inflection. From the printed page, get a clear idea of the meaning, and then follow the sense *mentally*, disregarding the mechanical marks of punctuation. These are usually put there to indicate the sentence elements, not for vocal guidance.

Take every opportunity to read such fine narrative poetry as *The Idyls of the King*.

Take time to read aloud some of the plays assigned for other purposes.

TOPICS FOR DISCUSSION

1. Discuss the importance of the voice in acting.
2. In training the voice would you emphasize the *Time-Pitch-Force-Quality* scheme, or would you simplify?
3. Explain the function of the diaphragm.
4. Is the actor altogether concerned with his fellows on the stage, or should he remember the audience vocally?
5. In reading lines, what would you say are the most important things to remember?
6. How is the emotional element of your dialogue expressed?
7. How does the amateur usually differentiate between reading and speaking?
8. How can you judge you have learned to *speak* your lines?
9. Why should you listen carefully to the speech that precedes the lines you are speaking?
10. Are all marks of punctuation to be vocally observed, or is the meaning of the sentence a better guide?

CHAPTER VII

TRAINING THE ACTORS

STAGE BUSINESS

The actor, in common with all other speakers, can use two kinds of language, the audible, and the visible—speech and action. The two naturally overlap, but speech is the expression of thought, and action is the manifestation of feeling. Speech is intellectual; action, emotional. Accordingly, although the actor needs a keen, alert mind, his best powers are in a free, responsive body. On the stage actions speak louder than words.

Our language may be thought of as a civilized attempt to explain the stimuli which first register as bodily reactions. In this order, acting is in effect only pantomime accompanied by speech.

Pantomime is the natural response to emotions, and constitutes the visible element in acting. Speech follows as the audible comment on these responses. To be entirely convincing, and artistically expressive, these two elements must be perfectly synchronized. The word must be suited to the action, and the action to the word.

In the way of simple nature, a man gets a sense impression (sensation), classifies it in his own mind (*idea or concept*), and there the process may stop. This process is carried a step farther in the arts. Having the sensation and the intellectual response, the artist seeks the most appropriate form in which to perpetuate or embody his experience. If he hap-

86

pens to be a musician, he chooses the purely audible medium of sounds. The sculptor selects the visible of mass; the painter, the visible in color. The dramatist chooses a form appealing to both ear and eye, and combines all other forms in producing its effects.

Having considered the audible interpretation in the preceding chapter, the visible phase, somewhat ambiguously called Stage Business, will now be considered.

Under this head we may discuss:

Action, in the sense of Gesture,

Deportment, in the sense of stage etiquette, and

Stage Business, in the sense of positions and movements on the stage.

Action is a word often used in a broad sense, to include gesture and stage business. Here we are to think of it in its more personal application. It designates the actor's manner of expressing himself on the stage. Such commonplace acts as walking, sitting down, rising, posing, assume an eloquence on the stage. They indicate character, personality, state of mind.

Bodily postures and movements help to arouse, as well as to express, corresponding vocal and emotional responses. The James-Lange theory of emotion has a practical application to the actor's art. Posture and movement *do,* in some subtle way, stimulate feeling, even though action be recognized as the natural effect of feeling. As Browning says, "Nor soul helps flesh more, now, than flesh helps soul." (Rabbi Ben Ezra) In this connection the actor should remember that *just as bodily response to stimuli precedes thinking about it, so action precedes speech by a barely perceptible interval.*

Pantomime, like tone language, has the advantage of being universally understood. Anybody who can see can understand. Words have a changeable, local meaning. What Sophocles, Plautus, or Chaucer said is understood in the original only by specialists in languages. Presumably, tone and action have been speaking the same language since man's beginning. We need not speak French to understand a Bernhardt in *Camille,* or Russian to follow the Moscow Art Theatre players in *The Cherry Orchard.* Training in pantomime consists of teaching the conscious agents of expression to act without interference from the unconscious. Practice in comic pantomime is one of the best ways to develop freedom and spontaneity on the stage.

Action is of two types: Definite and Indefinite. Definite action is prescribed by the author as necessary to the situations, or required by the context, such as calling on the telephone, picking up a pistol, closing a door. This is better classified as stage business, and will be discussed fully under that head. Indefinite action is invented by the actor, or by the director, to aid interpretation, characterization, or effect. A good actor spends as much time seeking motives for a large variety of personal action as he does studying his lines. In his inventiveness, he must take care to be true to nature. His action must be consistent with his make believe circumstance, with his assumed character, and with human nature in general.

Gesture is merely a very personal form of pantomime. It cannot be taught successfully, but it can be cultivated through many kinds of physical exercise like dancing and calisthenics.

Every good gesture consists of three distinct but

continuous movements: the preparation, the stroke, and the release. These have been variously named, but there is no question that they are inherent in every expressive gesture. The meaning of the sentence gives the impulse to action. A certain word in the sentence carries the burden of meaning. Toward this word, the gesture would naturally rise, on it spend its force, and from it gradually recover. Given the impulse to gesture, without the preparation and the release, the action would be abrupt and ineffective. It would lack the rhythm that every motion should have. The climax of the impulse is the stroke; the preparation and the release are the flow and ebb of it.

Excessive gesticulation is natural to the weak *thinker* and strong *feeler*. The best actors express themselves in a few discriminating gestures. Listen to what they say:

"Save the more emphatic movements for the more emphatic situations."—*George Arliss.*

"Eliminate every unessential movement of the head and hands, and avoid unnatural facial expression."—*John W. Cope.*

"Do not move about too much or you will lose ground."—*Robert MacLean.*

"With gesture as with everything else, the less you do of it the better."—*Louis Calvert.*

"Gesture to be effective must be significant, and to be significant it must be rare."—*George Henry Lewis.*

Nervous movements *in character* may be effective in portraying the character, but nervous movements in the actor's own person are fatal to effectiveness. Gesture is not called for by *every* state of mind; it should be saved for the dramatically important states. Every valuable gesture is the result of a strong desire to communicate thought and feeling. A poorly motivated gesture is not only untrue to nature, but it is extremely wasteful of the attention of the audience, the economy of which is one of the actor's chief concerns. A bad gesture is one in which only one set of muscles take part; a good gesture enlists the whole body.

A mannerism—always bad unless it belongs to characterization—is an impulse to gesture which is always arrested at the same point. Fingers habitually in the vest pocket, fingers of one hand constantly playing with a ring on the finger of the other hand, or hands carried limply at the waist, are three mannerisms most common to amateurs, and most difficult to cure.

The Hands.—When not actually employed to express thought and feeling, the hands should hang easily at the sides. The good actor suggests repose, and the hands have a good deal to do with this impression. An expressively reposeful hand is a sign of social poise in everyday life, and of poised self-confidence on the stage.

Abnormal states of mind call for abnormal use of hands, as well as of feet, head, and torso. Portrayal of character, too, makes an exception of all principles of normal action.

When an actor enters carrying something in his hands, he should seek a motive for ridding himself of the encumbrance at once. His hands should be freed for expressing emotional reactions. If the object carried helps him to do this, he should make use of it. A bashful swain, for instance, can express his peculiar state of mind and feeling by twisting a cap out of all semblance to itself. Deprived of it at entrance, he might be at a loss for other means of expressing himself.

It is the *palm* that does the speaking in a hand gesture. The fingers clinched over the palm may have a special meaning, but normally such a hand would express repression, and would indicate poor co-ordination. Most important of all, the hand is a part of the arm, and any hand movement must flow out of the motion of the whole arm.

Deportment.—Deportment is a word used to designate action of the personal type. The stage has its own code of behavior. An actor's behavior is modified by the presence of other actors on the stage, but not by any regard for the proprieties in respect to the audience. Hamlet's actions differ in the presence of Ophelia, in the presence of the King, and in the presence of Horatio, or Polonius. The audience across the footlights does not influence him in the least.

If a young man is playing the role of a gentleman, he will take off his hat as he comes into the presence of ladies on the stage; if he is playing the part of the boor, he will not. The ladies in the audience do not influence him in either case.

Stage Business.—Stage business is a term used to cover all movements on the stage, including entrances and exits, changes in position of actors, use of properties and furniture, stage pictures and tableaus, and all kinds of personal action. This may be planned for any or all of the following effects:

1. Bringing out character traits: Mrs. Cagle smoking a pipe in *Sun-Up*.
2. Establishing atmosphere, or creating a mood; watchmen in the first scene in *Hamlet*.

3. Illustrating content: Antony holding up Caesar's coat in *Julius Caesar*.
4. Controlling attention: in long speeches interspersing appropriate movement for the sake of variety.
5. Securing balance or emphasis: any kind of unobtrusive shift of positions of the actors on the stage.
6. Making comedy: any exaggerated, burlesque action that may beget a laugh.
7. Foreshadowing: doing some seemingly insignificant thing which may be forcefully recalled later on.

The Purpose of stage business is a dual one:
First, To Interpret the Story.
Second, To Create Interest.

Its appeal is to the eye, but it serves to reinforce the actor's speech by carrying meanings as well as interest. All business is planned in relation to the magnetic center of the stage, and the observation center of the auditorium. Our stage is assumed to be a room with four walls and a ceiling. The proscenium wall is assumed to be absent for the convenience of the audience. Although the modern actor is not over conscious of this missing partition, still he consciously conducts himself so as to be seen to best advantage by those on the other side of the absent wall.

There are no inviolable rules to be laid down for stage business, yet there are some well defined ways of bringing desired effects. These are governed by principles that may be systematized into a working code, and applied with an eye to frequent exceptions.

Like any other art, the stage is governed by the general principles of *Unity, Coherence,* and *Emphasis.* Unity is evident in the concentration of the whole picture to bring singleness of impression; coherence would be the carefully integrated movements of the actors in an uninterrupted advance toward the outcome; emphasis involves the centering of attention on emphatic characters and emphatic spots on the stage. Unity of purpose, coherence of movement, and emphasis of position, then, are the aims.

In their application to the stage picture, these principles are not to be considered separately. They may be inherently separate, but they are so inextricably involved in the application, that any attempt to keep them distinct would be confusing.

Let an imaginary line divide the stage into two parts: right center and left center. Other imaginary lines or circles may further divide into smaller units of space called acting *orbits.* Then the fewer the number of actors on the stage at any given time, the larger the orbit each may occupy. An actor is free to work out any interesting personal business within his own orbit, but he must not encroach upon another's space assignment, unless he is to exchange orbits with him for a good reason. Attention to this rule prevents huddling, preserves balance, and forestalls awkward interference.

Interest of the audience naturally focuses on the artistic center of the stage, a little to left of center. Around this spot the most important characters should be grouped, and the most significant business should take place. Side orbits are reserved for the less important characters and the less emphatic supporting action.

Characters may be judged according to three standards.

1. The *intrinsic* value. A character is interesting, not because of his importance to the story, but because of his unique personality. He would be as interesting outside of the story as in it.
2. The *conventional* value. Here interest centers not in personality, not in individuality. not in plot value, but in the character's extrinsic social prominence, his rank, position, political power, often unearned and undeserved.
3. The *emotional* value usually rests with the protagonist, the one to whom the story belongs, around whom the plot revolves, and in whose fortunes the audience is interested.

To illustrate from Hamlet.
The intrinsic would be represented by Polonius.
The conventional, by the King.
The emotional, by Hamlet.
The emotional value naturally takes precedence over the other two. Hamlet deserves to be emphatic whenever he appears on the scene, but there may be *moments* in the scene when either the King or Polonius may rightly claim the focus of attention, while Hamlet is gathering emotional force out of the scene. Thus, his temporary subordination emphasizes his permanent importance.

Sometimes during the progress of a play, a character may take on, in turn, all three values. Lear starts out with the conventional, falls to the level of the intrinsic, but retains the emotional throughout. Fully aware of this shifting emphasis, the actor learns how, and when, to take the stage, and how to relinquish the limelight in favor of another.

In assigning actors to their respective orbits, it is well to follow, in an irregular way, the arc of a circle described by a compass, with its pivot in the center of the auditorium. Two actors on the stage would face each other from opposite sides of the center line. Three actors would be so placed as to form a triangle with the most important character at the apex at center upstage. As other actors might appear they would be fitted into this irregular arc line in such a way as to secure balance and preserve emphasis.

It is most important in arranging the stage picture to avoid the semblance of geometric precision. There must always be an unstudied, informal irregularity in following the dial of the compass. The purpose in following it at all is to keep the *picture open to the audience.*

Crowds are to be arranged according to the principles of emphasis, balance, rhythm, and line. The balance may be in number, or in *weight.* Hamlet alone outweighs a mob. Antony on one half of the stage *balances* a mob of angry citizens on the other half. This is one method of *emphasis.* Another way might be to put Antony in the center, and the mob on all sides.

In the trial scene in *The Merchant Of Venice,* Shylock, the emotional value, remains emphatically alone during the progress of the trial. When the tables turn on him, the alignment dissolves and he is uncomfortably enmeshed.

The following *do's* and *dont's* may be helpful to both actors and directors, if they are properly evaluated and carefully applied. They are intended as helpful hints to amateurs, not as inviolable rules.

1. Learn to *pretend* so thoroughly that it ceases to be pretense, both to yourself and the audience.

2. The best principles for any art are those that bring the desired effect. Try to bring something original into your work.

3. If you have so much as killed a fly in anger, you have the foundation for a murder scene. Let your imagination do the rest.

4. In rehearsal you practice for team-work. Work out your interpretation in the privacy of your study.

5. Live your part, but first understand the part you are to live.

6. If you would learn to *act* effectively, first learn to *listen* well.

7. Help direct the attention of the audience to an emphatic speech by attending to it intensely yourself.

8. Exhibit a plausible *motive* for everything you do and say. If you say nothing more than *Oh,* let the audience understand why you are exclaiming.

9. Keep your distance. A good rule to prevent huddling is to keep at arm's length from your neighbor, unless emotion brings you closer.

10. Whenever any part of the picture shifts, shift with it so as to re-establish balance.

11. Sit, rise, or move on the right word of your speech. A transitional speech often calls for movement. This, like a good gesture, must be exactly timed. The key word in the sentence may be emphasized by a climax of movement.

12. *Stand Still.* Do not so much as lift a heel from the floor unless it means something. The longer you hold your position, the stronger you grow in it.

13. When you have a certain position to reach on the stage, it is often best to move toward it in a straight line, not by detour.

14. On a large stage, before a large audience, play as much as possible in front of the furniture. On a small stage this is not so important.

15. Unless you have a very good reason for it, do not move while another is speaking.

16. If you and another actor have the same prescribed business, break up the simultaneity of it. If both are to rise, one should move slightly ahead of the other. So with walking in the same direction, sitting, or leaving the stage. The uniformity of a drill is to be avoided, unless that is the effect desired.

17. The actor speaking may cross in front of another of whatver rank or sex. The rule that a gentleman never crosses in front of a lady does not hold on the stage. You should, even though speaking, cross *behind* another, if he is seated. But never cross in front of another, if he is speaking. Professional directors disregard this rule constantly. Sometimes with good effect, more often with bad. In a recent production of *Personal Appearance,* for instance, an actor stood directly in front of a seated woman *while she was speaking.* Here the actor, in an effort to achieve utter informality, disregarded the rights of the audience to an almost unforgivable degree.

18. Do not move during the delivery of an important line, either by yourself or another. Movement of any kind attracts attention, and is liable to minimize the effect of the speech.

19. When an actor has occasion to step in front of you, step in the opposite direction at the instant of crossing. This will expedite the re-adjustment.

Besides, *opposition* is a law of rhythm, and a fundamental law of all art.

20. Make turning toward the audience an early and thoroughly established habit. It is usually as easy to turn with the face down-stage as up, and it is much more effective. This rule, too, is often disregarded on the professional stage. Where it adds to rhythm and variety of movement, the effect is pleasing. If it has no artistic motive, the effect is a feeling of audience neglect.

21. Work out to the full limits of the stage. Spread your picture on as large a canvas as your frame affords.

22. Avoid stepping backward, unless you are retreating in fear. Normally, it is better to turn and walk forward for a step or two.

23. Whenever you have anything to express, be sure that the audience sees your agents of expression—face, eyes, chest.

24. The chest is the seat of your personality and the center of control. Let the chest lead. Make your movements, gestures, and poses with chest toward the audience. To be sure, there are exceptions. The back may speak most eloquently on occasion, like Olga Nethersole's in *Labyrinth*.

25. Cultivate carriage, posture, grace, and ease of motion. If you keep your weight on the balls of your feet, you will suggest life and lightness.

26. "Do not forget that the eyes play an important part in acting."—*Robert MacLean*. Your eyes are responsible for much of your effectiveness on the stage. Learn to use them.

27. Focus the attention on an important speaker by listening to him attentively. This means looking at him, if the nature of the content makes it nat-

ural for you to do so. We often listen attentively
with averted eyes. Such an attitude often implies
more than a steady stare.

28. Where to look is a fine point in acting. Ob-
stinacy, refusal, shame, reminiscence—all are best
expressed with averted eyes. A chatty conversation
calls for an easily shifting objective. Many speeches
are thrown on the air for anybody to catch.

29. Cultivate an intense, interested look. Keep
your eyes wide open, and hold them steadily on a
level with the eyes of other actors.

30. Amateurs often, after delivering a speech,
prematurely turn to the next speaker as if to say,
"That's your cue; go ahead." This is the surest
sign of inexperience on the stage. Let each take
care of his own cues. If the nature of your speech
has made it natural for you to turn away, don't
turn back again until he has said something to draw
your eyes, or until your next direct speech requires
you to do so. Study carefully the habits of actual
life, and transfer them to your work on the stage.

31. In general, all eyes are on the speaker, even
though he himself may not be looking at anyone
in particular.

32. Look where you are going, and go where you
are looking.

33. In making an emphatic entrance, come down
where all can see you. The actor, presenting his
chest squarely to the audience, makes the most
effective entrance.

34. In a group entrance, the speaker enters last.
As a result, he speaks toward his partners as well
as toward the audience.

35. Enter with life and exit with life. Pick up the

audience as you come on, and take them with you as you leave.

36. If you happen to be a butler or servant answering a call, or announcing a guest, enter only one step or two and stand at attention.

37. Plan your speeches near your exit cue so that you speak the last words at the door, and move toward the exit on appropriate transitional lines. Attention to this rule is very important. It improves coherence by eliminating the blank interval between the last word and the exit. An example of a plausible exception might be a character of such intrinsic interest, or in such a state of mind, that the silent movement across the stage would speak louder than words.

38. Learn to do *nothing* effectively.

39. Try to invent bits of business to point the human nature of your role.

40. Cultivate the habit of referring all personal business to the up-stage and down-stage lines. In facing right or left, the up-stage arm is extended in gesture, the up-stage foot is advanced in pose, the down-stage knee touches the floor in kneeling, the man's down-stage arm is below, his up-stage arm above the woman's in embracing.

41. In the stage embrace, there should be no effect of tenseness, except for comic effect, perhaps. The lady yields gracefully, the man supports her with strong tenderness.

42. The stage kiss may be a sham, and yet look real. Turn the faces so that they appear to meet, but do not. Study the movies for the stage kiss, and then avoid most of what you see. The real kiss is often objectionable to amateurs. It is also the cause

of much bitterness, jealousy, and divorce in professional circles.

43. The classic stage bow, now used only in burlesque or Shakespeare, is made by bringing the right arm sweepingly to the head, swinging the hat widely out and up to the left breast, at the same time bowing from the hips. The corresponding feminine *dip* is easily achieved, but the more profound curtsey of the minuet age must be carefully practiced.

44. Fainting and falling are matters of personal accomplishment. You may learn to fall effectively in your own fashion, but the safest way for the beginner is to kneel, sit, and lie in such rapid succession that there is the illusion of a swift collapse. A man may fall in any direction; a woman with head toward the audience, unless she is dressed in masculine attire, as skirts cannot be depended upon to behave as they should.

45. Cultivate *repose*, at the same time seeking motives for a variety of interesting action. You can learn to light a cigar, warm your hands at the fireplace, or open a book with poise.

"After all repose is what we all aim for."—*Louis Calvert*. Keep your "gentlemanly reserve," but don't be afraid to act. *Abandon* is worth a great deal to a young actor, that is, abandon in repose.

46. Work up to the most exciting part of the play so that it may come as a climax. If you arrive too abruptly, the audience may lose the thrill that comes from satisfied suspense.

47. Take some initiative. Don't wait for the director to push you into every position, or draw out of you the meaning of every speech. If you over act, he will be only too happy to tone you down. It is

easier to eliminate superfluities than to build up inadequacies.

48. Watch the development of others, and you will profit.

49. Never promise the director that you will improve on the night of the performance. He wants to see you do the best you can now.

50. Don't damage illusion by letting any of the audience see you in the wings ready for your cue.

51. Lose yourself in your part. So long as you are conscious of acting, you will be amateurishly ineffective.

52. Better play too fast than too slow; better to violate the natural pace than run the risk of dragging.

53. In a telephone conversation, give the other party time for his part. The audience hears the audible end, they must be allowed to imagine the unheard part of the conversation.

54. Don't ask the director the reason for each bit of direction. Try to figure it out yourself.

55. Take up your cues promptly, but not too promptly. The time between speeches is a part of their meaning. Cultivate a sense of the psychological moment. In a scene of rapid action, the cues would be snapped up quickly. In scenes of thoughtful deliberation, a great deal of hesitancy may be in order. The *visible* response to cues, however, is always instantaneous. The eyes, face, body speak at once; the words may come after the appropriate mental process has taken place. *Action precedes speech by a perceptible interval.*

56. *Stand still,* while you are standing; *move positively* when you move.

57. Talk as naturally as you do off-stage, but three or four times more effectively.

58. *Exhibit a clear motive for all you do and say.*

59. *Practice,* practice, and then again, *Practice.*

ASSIGNMENT

Practice on assigned roles is to be carried on extensively in connection with this chapter. An unlimited amount of time can be profitably devoted to this assignment. Chapters VI, VII and VIII may be used as a basis for a whole semester's course in acting.

As you have opportunity to watch good professional productions, watch the stage business closely and compare it with the suggestions given above, noting when it has the desired effect, and when it appears to neglect the audience unnecessarily.

TOPICS FOR DISCUSSION

1. Discuss the relative values of intellect and feeling in any acted role.
2. Which predominates in drama, mind or heart?
3. Draw a distinction, if any, between *Action* and *Stage Business.*
4. Discuss the two types of Action.
5. Analyze a good gesture.
6. How can you reconcile poise with abandon?
7. It may be said that the best actors behave and speak with "sublime simplicity." Explain the statement. Is it true?
8. Explain the dual purpose of Stage Business.
9. How do you apply Unity, Coherence, Emphasis to the Stage?
10. Discuss the magnetic center of the stage.
11. How may *balance* be achieved?
12. Are there any rules given in this chapter that you would challenge? Do so.

CHAPTER VIII

TRAINING THE ACTORS

CHARACTERIZATION

Acting is representing not only make-believe situations but also make-believe people. We speak of straight parts and character parts. Strictly considered, they are all character parts. No one will pay admission to see the actor's own personality on the stage.

The actor is always someone else. The hardest role to make convincing is usually one that makes the smallest demands for qualities outside the actor's own person. Franklin Sargent expected of the actor:

1. *A good physique.* This is not necessarily a good figure, but a healthy, free, and responsive body.

2. *A nervous emotional temperament.* A phlegmatic disposition is doomed to failure on the stage. Nervousness, well controlled, is a decided advantage.

3. *An active imagination.* Imagination is a sine qua non in acting. Joseph Jefferson placed feeling and imagination above every other gift. David Belasco named imagination, supported by several other qualities as the secret of success on the stage. E. H. Sothern recognizes imagination as the prime requisite of good acting, and Mrs. Fiske tells us that the actor is exactly as big as his imagination. Imagination is an asset everywhere, but in acting it is everything.

4. *Theatric instinct.* This is the knack of showing off to advantage. It is the innate, or cultivated, sense

of doing the right thing, the most effective thing, at all times.

5. *Dramatic intelligence.* This is the power to create situations in all their causal relationships, and the instinctive perception of, and response to, dramatic motivation.

The actor is a creator. Shakespeare created Hamlet, but for three centuries that heroic figure has slumbered between the pages of a book. It is only when a Booth, or a Sothern, or John Gielgud is inspired with the glorious possibilities of the role, that Hamlet begins to breathe and speak, and castigate himself into action.

"Creativeness begins from the moment when in the soul of the actor there appears a magical-creative IF,—the *imagined* truth in which the actor can believe as sincerely and with greater enthusiasm than he believes practical truth."—Stanislavski.

"The actor borrows from the author, from stage tradition, from his own stock of knowledge of men, women, and things, from his general experience, and from his imagination. He sees his part and grasps it. It does not belong to him, but he inhabits its body. . . . The true actor can take up his part at any time and instinctively incite the desired effect. He commands us to weep, laugh, shiver, fear. . . . He does not wait until he experiences these emotions himself, or for grace from above to enlighten him."—Coquelin.

Impersonation Is a Creative Art.—Every acted role is, in effect, an uncovering and an embodying of hidden virtues and vices, of mental habits and physical idiosyncrasies, of secret passions and ambitions. It is the act of putting human nature into the physical, both in its individual manifestation, and in its universal implication. To the student the practice of impersonation may be of great value aside from the direct bearing on the art of acting. It may aid him in his struggle against selfconsciousness in public. It requires intense concentration, and concentration banishes self-awareness.

In the theatre the actor uses everybody and everything for his field of research, and nowhere is imagination more important than in characterization. Characters are conceived through it; moods are realized through it; beauty, sympathy, passion, are re-created through it. To be set down as a good character actor, then, is as high a compliment as can be paid an actor.

There is one very subtle element in character portrayal that is often missed by the careless or incompetent actor. That is, the universal implications mentioned in a preceding paragraph. The mediocre actor may succeed in presenting the individual, but the great artist shows the individual plus a universal reality that suggests eternal human nature. It is really the *art* of characterization that we admire on the stage. A real tramp would be about as interesting before the footlights as he is when he appears at the back door. But if the student watches him while he is being fed, and then through his own person represents what he has observed, his art will excite admiration and approval. The more detailed and minute the observation, and the more faithful the delineation of the traits observed, the better his portrayal will be.

It is hard to define just what happens in good character acting. The artist must be himself and the character at one and the same time. He does not exactly *adopt* the form and manner. He rather grows into them, and expresses *himself* through them. James Barton, representing a drunk trying to make his way into a speak-easy, is his sober self all the time, yet his character is gloriously drunk, even to the very independent way in which his little finger behaves.

In preparing for your character role:

1. Study actual people as well as fictitious types. Often a characterization by a fine actor may help.

2. Organize and synchronize yourself with the part. If you have the role of a queen, for instance, practice queenly bearing in your daily behavior. Walk, sit, stand, talk like a queen. Get into any other type in the same way. Learn the habits of your character intimately, and then practice the habits off the stage as well as on. The stately attitude of the colonial dame may be felt by holding the arms gracefully folded above the waist, with feet together. Her movements may be imitated through the practice of the minuet.

3. Every character has some *master gesture*, as well as some prominent mannerism of speech. Practice this gesture until it becomes an unconscious part of you.

4. Every character has a tempo of its own, showing mentality and temperament. Try to sense these, and then adapt your speech and action to them.

5. Do not depend upon make-up to help you realize your character. Make the character a part of yourself first, and then your make-up will be all the more consistent. You do not need wrinkles and a gray beard to practice the wide base and the shuffling gait of old age. You do not need bi-focals to suggest the presbyopic difficulties in seeing objects.

Tilting the head and holding the object away is all that is necessary in practice.

6. Be in character all the time. In general, you can help yourself to a more vivid realization of your character by:

The way you pronounce your words.

Understanding human nature in general, and the nature of your character in particular.

Analyzing your part in detail, studying the parts separately, then putting them together again for unity of effect.

Determining the general traits first, then particularizing.

Determining national traits as well as individual. The Russian peasant, for instance, has the age-long habit of crossing himself and bowing servilely at the slightest provocation.

Studying the history of your character: race, nationality, social position, historic period, physical type, economic status.

Finding portraits of your character type and noting every feature in turn: face, neck, hands, waist, feet.

Studying living types: their walk, talk, play of features, expression around the eyes, manner of sitting, standing, rising.

Learn your character as you learn good or bad manners.

Whatever the motion pictures may lack, they have given us some remarkable character portraits. To be sure, portraits just as good are to be found on the contemporary stage, but the contemporary stage may not be available to all of us.

The thought, language, and character are the

author's; emotion and representation in visible form
are the actor's. Just as the author takes notes in
preparation for his composition, so the actor must
observe, and take mental notes in preparation for
his portrait. Practice must precede performance, as
life-long habits precede living. The actor must learn
the theory, the principles, the objectives of his art.
But these are worthless to him unless, through constant practice, he has learned to apply them. He
first learns to *know*; then he learns to *do*.

It is as strange as it is true, that in order to be
able to make an awkward gesture in character, you
must first be able to make a graceful one naturally.
To have perfect control of your character at every
stage of the performance, you must first have perfect
control of yourself. Acting is more than imitation,
more than miming. "It is a kind of re-birth, a shift
in multiple personality, the capture of an elusive
ego."

In good art, thought is dominant; in poor art, the
material stands out. This suggests a caution: the
material for characterization—voice, body, language
—must be subservient to thought and feeling. Character portrayal is only one phase of the art of the
stage. It is one of the visible forms, and it carries
its own content and significance. Every character
must bear its true relation to the total meaning and
effect of the play as a whole.

"Experience in character teaches much about acting and about self."

—Stark Young.

Costuming and make-up are a part of characterization, and a decidedly important part. Being of a
mechanical nature, however, they properly fall un-

der the second part of this text. There each will have a chapter to itself.

Exercises

In order to get the *feel* of throwing off your own personality and taking on another, follow out this schedule until you have achieved a distinct character portrayal:

1. Find a striking character type among the people you have known. For first practice, a very broad type is the best.

2. Study your subject until you feel that you know his inner motives, as well as his outward appearance. Get at the secret of his mental and emotional characteristics, then practice his physical manifestations.

3. Keep your attention on the mental picture you have formed of him. Forget everything else. Who you are, where you are, and what you might think and feel should be temporarily forgotten.

4. Do not rest until you feel a motive for every posture and every movement. Study how the body affects the mind, the mind, body.

5. Start working from a perfectly relaxed attitude of body and mind. You cannot expect to force yourself into the foreign mould, but you can easily coax yourself into it by degrees.

6. At first try silent posture and pantomime; later add speech.

7. Next try putting your character into an imagined situation, perhaps into something like the environment where you first found him.

8. When you have successfully represented several subjects from life, you may attempt the more elusive folk of literature.

Can you visualize: Mr. Pickwick? Mr. Winkle? Scrooge? Juliet's Nurse? Touchstone? Be sure you attempt any of these only after you have been steeped in them.

Points for Discussion

1. Discuss Sargent's physical requirements for the actor.
2. What does the actor do when he enacts a character role?

3. What is the *master* gesture?
4. Outline one good method of getting the *feel* of your character.
5. Where can you go to *learn* your character?
6. Can you point out any national difference between: A Norwegian and a Swede? A Russian and a Spaniard?
7. Is old make-up all you need for representing a very old man? What else?
8. What can *talkies* teach of characterization?
9. Of what disciplinary value may practice in characterization be?
10. Describe a character from life in all his peculiar traits.

CHAPTER IX

ORDER OUT OF CHAOS

Directing and producing plays is such an exacting, time-consuming, nerve-racking business that few people would care to engage in it simply for the doubtful livelihood it might afford. Something more than the promise of subsistence prompts the director to sacrifices which a layman could not be made to understand. This is the *creative "if"* Stanislavski speaks of.

The director is a creator, who probably works seven nights out of the week. During the progress of his labor, he may smile for the sake of morale. If all goes well, along about the fortieth rehearsal, his timid smile becomes a genuine grin, which grows as he views his handiwork. He looks at what he has done, and sees *that it is good*.

Order out of chaos! This is what he has been waiting for, working for. His patience, perseverance, industry have been rewarded. The director alone, who has taken up a freshly assembled amateur cast, patiently molded the plastic human clay, depressing a peak here, raising a valley there, smoothing a sharp crag, or felling an exuberant tree, knows the joy that comes when order begins to emerge. He has shaped a seemingly hopeless bundle of conflicting personalities into a symphony of speech and action.

Just as the cook, by some uncanny art of divination, knows when her pot has stewed long enough, so the director knows instinctively when his rehearsals begin to show signs of the finished product. A new confidence has taken possession of the members of the cast. A kind of surprised zest has entered into their work. What has been mostly drudgery up to this point suddenly becomes great fun. The actors have at last entered into the world of make-believe, and lost themselves in it. When this result has once been attained, the director ceases to worry. He knows that no matter how uninspired any subsequent rehearsal may be, all will be well in the end. He can confidently set a date for the final rehearsal.

The Dress Rehearsal.—The ideal dress rehearsal is yet to be held. To the experienced director it does not matter much whether the rehearsal is ideal or otherwise. He does not intend it to be a smooth production. By its very purpose it needs to be a carefully calculated meting out of space and clothing, of acquainting the actors with the final detail of their properties and environment, and of working out kinks in the more obstinate scenes. If the cast has once reached an unbroken, climactic, quickened performance in any previous rehearsal, they can be depended upon to do it again before an audience. If the dress rehearsal has resulted in complete understanding of every detail of the production by every member of the cast and staff, it may be regarded as satisfactory, whether the acting be good, bad, or indifferent.

The wise director has taken the precaution to concentrate his main effort in the first part of the rehearsal season. He can then allow his actors a little breathing space toward the end. It does not pay to be behind schedule on rehearsals, so that a hectic final spurt is necessary. Actors do better work after a rest of a day or two, than if they have to go full throttle to the last minute.

The main purpose of the dress rehearsal is to get everything laid out accurately. Colors in gowns must be harmonized, unexpected obstructions in the setting removed. If the director is fortunate enough to have his own theatre, he can hold as many rehearsals in full dress and setting as he thinks profitable. But to make repeated dress rehearsals valuable, he should invite a few guests to stimulate the actors.

There is one superstition concerning dress rehearsals which should be disregarded. This is the common belief among actors that a poor dress rehearsal indicates a good final performance, and vice versa. This notion has come about because too few people realize what constitutes a good dress rehearsal. Even the members of the cast often wonder why the director can remain so calm when everything is going so badly. But the director is satisfied if he has succeeded in getting the mechanical details into working order. He can pretty well trust his human agents to rise to the occasion, even if they have not gone through their lines and business uninterrupted, and with zest. In the proper sense of the word, a *good* dress rehearsal is absolutely necessary to a satisfactory final performance.

The Final Performance.—The public performance of an amateur play is its own reward. Tonight the drudgery of the tedious weeks of preparation is forgotten, and all is joy and hopeful expectancy. There are few experiences in life comparable to that of casting a spell over a large audience, kindling their emotions, exciting their mirth. No wonder young people are willing to forego so many pleasant things in college life for the sake of taking part in a play.

There are a few general hints that should be noted in regard to the public performance. Every member of the cast must be at the theatre at the specified hour. There are many things to be done, and no one has a right to cause any anxiety by a delayed arrival. The curtain must go up on the advertised hour, and since few amateurs can be trusted to put on their own make-up, there must be time for careful, un-hurried touching up of all the members of the cast by an expert. There may be unexpected hitches in wardrobes, or properties, which are not serious, if discovered in time. Brought to light at the last min-ute by a tardy arrival, such things throw everything into confusion.

Every member of the staff should be happy and cheerful. This is no time for anxiety and gloom. The director is the calmest and most cheerful of all. He must radiate confidence and composure. A nervous, excitable person, who goes to pieces under the strain of putting on a play, would be happier in some other profession. Several minutes before the curtain goes up, the director calls the cast to the stage and looks them over. He lines them up so as to get the total effect of the picture, he checks up on their clothing and make-up, and he corrects any sagging in physi-cal or mental attitude. Having satisfied himself that all are ready and "rarin' to go," he sends them to their places with words of flattery and encourage-ment.

Different duties have been delegated to different individuals. The careful director checks up on them all. He makes sure that the scene shifters are prop-erly instructed, that the electrician has his lighting effects well in hand, that the property man has all the necessary articles in place, that the orchestra has been furnished with the musical score, that ushers are on the job, with instructions as to the presentation of flowers.

A good prompter is a great comfort at the final performance. He should be superfluous, so far as prompting actors on forgotten lines is concerned, and in a well coached play he usually is, but he is very important in other ways. He sees that all actors are ready for their entrances, that bells are rung at the proper time, and that all off-stage noises coincide with the requirements of the dialogue.

The director may relieve himself of a great deal of worry and work if he appoints and properly instructs a competent stage manager, who can take over most of the back-stage duties.

Final hints to college actors: Don't get the notion that it is your duty or privilege to ape professional stage folk in your personal conduct. Any form of misconduct is more serious in a college or school group than in any other type of organization. Professionals who come and go, who have no local reputation to sustain, may conduct their private lives without much regard to their public, *if they wish*. But amateurs, as members of a community, must be careful. If they expect the good will and patronage of the public, they must first deserve it.

There is that excitement about the stage that gets into the blood and works on the emotions in a subtle way. To young actors in the flush of this excitement, many things seem innocent and proper, which to fathers and mothers look rather grave. Parents look to the director for the decorous behavior of their children. Any breath of scandal concerning the director or any member of the cast or staff, may do irreparable damage to the cause of amateur dramatics in that community. More school directors have lost their jobs for allowing too much freedom than for any other one cause.

It is expected of amateur actors to be as happy and to get as much fun out of the game, as is consistent with good work and good conduct. But they should never fail in their respect for the moral code of the community in which they live and work.

Part Two
THE MECHANICAL ARTS

As no student is likely to have aptitude or interest in *all* branches of stagecraft, it might be well for the instructor to require special work of each student in the field he elects. The women will probably be interested in painting and costuming; the men in scene construction and electricity. In this way, the content of the course may be held to the academic standard without imposing tasks that might be so far outside the student's special ability as to be a waste of time.

CHAPTER X

SCENE DESIGNING

The theatre is a building or place with seats, and provided with a stage or open space upon which plays or dramatic spectacles are performed. It is a word derived from the Greek meaning *to view* or see.—*Encyclopedia Britannica.*

Because scene designing presupposes a knowledge of the theatre in all its phases of development, a bird's-eye view of the past is in order.

A complete survey of the subject would embrace architecture from earliest times to the present; the *stage* in its evolution from a simple open space to its present status of composite art; the *setting* from the early marble background to our elaborate *inscenierung*; *stage lighting* from the time that it employed the afternoon sun to our highly differentiated and mood-inducing electric display; *costuming* and *make-up* with their interesting history; *playwriting* in its changing traditions of form and content; and finally *acting* with its shifting styles and conventions.

The art of the theatre began in earnest in an open space in front of a tier of seats cut out of a convenient hillside. This Greek model is still copied where the topography and weather are favorable to outdoor performances.

Later this acting space became a platform pushed out among the audience so that the actors were exposed to flying vegetables from three sides. The fourth side formed the permanent background composed of drapery, lumber, or masonry, variously em-

121

bellished to add glamor to the picture. Gradually to this back wall were added side walls, at first as *wings* running in grooves parallel to the back wall, designated as first, second, third entrances right or left. Old copies of printed plays still remind us of this type of scenery by the use of such symbols as RUE, LLE, or 1RE, etc. These wings, together with the proscenium arch, which was added to further limit the acting space, give us the *picture-frame* stage. Finally, the open wing sets gave way to our realistic side walls and ceiling, and actual doors and windows. This we now call a *box set*.

Exterior scenes, until recently, consisted of conventionally painted wings and backdrops. Those whose impressionable youth thrilled to such scenery still have the same nostalgia for trees, lakes, rivers, palaces, or mountains painted on an artificially lighted backdrop. But this old method has generally been supplanted by the skydome with *cutouts*, and *raking-pieces* shaped and painted to represent natural features along the horizon line.

Thus, scene designing has become an art in its own right, and in turn has given rise to the arts of scene construction, scene-painting, stage lighting. All of these combine to enhance the beauty of the picture, and to suggest time, place, and mood more artistically. This department of the theatre has added many names to the hall of fame. Among these are Adolphe Appia, Max Reinhardt, Gordon Craig, Robert Jones, Lee Simonson, Norman Bel Geddes, and a score of others. Each name stands for some original theory of design, out of which may eventually emerge a more convincing and less obtrusive environment for the actor's art.

A Working Theory.—Alexander Bakshy says that
there is a new movement at work in the theatre today to return the stage to its old purpose of pure
make-believe. The idea of illusion in realism is being discounted, the theory being that the painted
sea or sky should stand for what they are *on the
stage* rather than for what they are in actuality.

The audience assembles in the theatre to play a
game. They are in a mood to say to the producer,
"Let's pretend." They are obliged to accept so many
things in the spirit of pretense, that they would
perhaps rather accept the rest in the same spirit.
They know, for instance, that when a player is shot
dead, he isn't dead at all, and that no *real* bullet
has passed through his body. If they thought that
stage pistols were loaded with real powder and ball,
they would immediately leave the theatre. They
have not come to see real bloodshed. They prefer
to be deceived in that, so why not in *all* respects?

The glory of Shakespeare is his eternal youth.
Most of his plays are veritable Lands of Oz for
grown-ups. Rosalind puts on masculine attire and
deceives Orlando with a flimsy disguise that would
not fool a real lover for two seconds. Yet the audience accepts the improbability without question, except those, perhaps, who are constituted similarly
to George Bernard Shaw. On the other hand, Ibsen's
plays appeal to reason. They have the effect of semi-
literalness, or a mixed figure of speech. Plays of extreme realism attempt to fool us into believing that
we are getting the *truth*, when we know perfectly
well we are not.

Bakshy divides the entire field of stage practice
into two methods:

The representational, or life on the stage *as it is*.

The presentational, or life as it is *on the stage.*

These two methods take in all the *-isms* that have sprung up in our day, none of which may hope to make the stage anything but what it is. The presentational method frankly admits it.

The consciousness of theatrical mechanism cannot be removed from the collective mind of the audience. A good play succeeds in making the audience forget the craft and lose themselves in the make-believe. The danger in modern stagecraft is that by trying to disguise the stage, and to make it something it is not fitted by nature to be, we make the audience more conscious of the mechanical nature of the process.

Bakshy's analysis points a lesson to the college amateur. The school is the right place for experimentation, and it is important that the right direction be given. Instead of futilely struggling to eliminate stage mechanics, why not concentrate on devising means of making the audience less conscious of them? To most of the audience a setting is just a setting. The first sight of it may arouse momentary admiration, or it may be so poorly done as to arouse disgust. In either case they lose track of the setting when a good actor takes the stage. If the good actor is not forthcoming, the set may remain in the foreground of their consciousness. If it does, either the play, the acting, or both are at fault. The play is the thing, and the scene designer must work to make it more beautifully and more emphatically so.

Scene Design.—The modern scene designer is as truly an artist as the painter of landscapes. His art is all the more exacting because it must be subservient to other arts to which it is subordinated. His chief aim must be to express the essential quality of

Note the unstudied balance in furniture and wall openings.

the play. At the same time he must create an adequate environment for the actor's interpretative moods and movements.

He may make his design representational, imitative of actual place, or symbolical, employing lines and a variety of color to induce mood and create atmosphere. A realistic play, like *A Doll's House*, calls for a literal representational setting. A fantasy like *Alice In Wonderland*, or *Beggar On Horseback*, demands a suitable decorative design. Any play of poetic imagination lends itself to the symbolic setting, and would be seriously weakened in its effect by a literal, representational scene design.

A scene laid in an ordinary interior makes little demand upon the designer beyond the simplified picture drawn according to the author's specifications, with original touches. The designer for the amateur stage must consider the local stage facilities. Purposeless decorative designs are detrimental. It is always better to suggest reality through simplification, than to imitate through multiplicity of detail.

Scenery is important only as it assists the actor by furnishing the necessary environment. It should serve to localize the action, suggest the nature of the story, and make as pleasing a picture as is consistent with proper emphasis on the story as told by the actors. The play is the important element in the combination, and the designer, with all other collaborating artists, must keep his part subordinate. The great temptation here, as elsewhere, is to practice designing for its own sake. The purpose of design is well emphasized in the following statements from authority:

"Scenery is the visual expression of the dynamic

spirit of the play in all that comes before the eye."
—*Gordon Craig*.

"Scenery is the light and those plastic elements
that add vitality to the actor's living presence."—
Adolphe Appia.

"Scenery is the creation of plastic forms and spaces
that are an integral part of acting, and project its
meaning." —*Lee Simonson*.

"Scenery is . . . the visualization in color, light,
and line of the dominant emotions."—*Kenneth
MacGowan*.

"Scenery is the actor's environment."—*Robert
Jones*.

A good test of the well designed set is that it does
not distract attention from the performance. In its
broadest sense, scenery is all that can be taken in
through the eye—walls, hangings, decorations, furniture, properties, costumes, and lighting effects.
The designer works all of these into his picture.

As student designers, you may proceed in this
manner. You first consult the author of the play.
What is the central idea? What type of play is it?
What locale does it call for? In what period of time
is it cast? What is the prevailing mood? This determined, you next consider what style of production
will suit it best.

1. *Realism:* representing actuality in every detail,
with four walls and a ceiling, and with furniture and
accessories true to life.

2. Simplified *Realism:* suggesting a great deal of
reality through careful selection of a few details.

3. *Symbolism:* using details that *connote* reality,
or which stimulate the imagination of the audience
to construct for itself convincing *unreality*. This is

particularly suited to plays of imaginative suggestiveness.

4. *Stylization:* carrying suggestion to the extreme of unreality in an attempt to induce a pronounced mood, and to reveal the artist's own response to the author's idea. This is best suited to fairy tales. It accentuates the spirit of play at the expense of the concrete mechanical nature of the stage.

5. *Formalism:* representing no definite locality, only picturing a vague environment emotionally suited to the spirit of the play, using isolated walls, pillars, steps, implying thereby that the *essence* of the play is more important than its physical body. It discards detailed setting and concentrates on the actor.

6. *Constructivism:* suggesting our mechanical age by use of skeletal structures, sharp angles gone wild, colossal wheels, trellises, scaffolds. This method is most favored in Russian design.

Plasticism, a three dimensional setting, *Cubism, Futurism, Expressionism,* and *Naturalism,* along with several other *isms* that have found their way into theatrical terminology, are so vague in their meaning, and so intervolved, as to be significant in name only. An original combination of these methods, or some happy selection from any of them, may bring something new to the stage. The best method is still to be found.

In designing for a college theatre, the funds available must be considered. A small budget will call for simplification, while sound financial backing may permit elaboration. The local stage, its space limitations, the height and width of the proscenium arch, the depth of the stage, the height of the gridiron, if any, the presence or absence of the cyclorama, the lighting equipment all must be considered, and may modify the artist's design.

You start by drawing the *ground plan*, the lines on the floor along which the walls are to be set.

Next draw your *elevation*, the scenery in upright position placed along the lines of the ground plan, and sketch in the doors and windows.

Finally, you make your *color sketch*, decorating the elevation with appropriate color combinations, sketching in furniture, fixtures, draperies, not neglecting the mood and atmosphere the play is to incite.

Investigate the effect of color on the audience, and the effect of artificial lighting on colors.

You study how to paint into your sketch the effect of rain, sun, laughter, tears, mystery, mischief, romance, virtue, vice, nobility, grandeur.

Strive for strength and simplicity of line, dynamic tone of color, and a feeling for action.

Try for such subtle exaggeration as will high-light the emphatic spots on the stage, and pull the best emotional response from the audience.

Your scene will be well designed if it is:

1. Expressive of the locality, thought, and spirit of the play.

2. Attractive to the eye without robbing the actors of the attention they must always command.

3. Capable of carrying the impression to the farthest part of the auditorium.

4. Adaptable to effective stage business.

5. Practicable in that it is easily built, quickly assembled, and readily shifted.

6. Harmonious, unifying all the elements into a singleness of impression.

Read a good play carefully. Determine what style of design would best fit its purpose and spirit. Is the play written realistically or symbolically?

First, take a realistic play like *A Doll's House* or *The First Mrs. Fraser*. Read carefully the author's specifications for the setting. Decide how far you wish to carry out the author's plan, and to what extent you want to be original. As the first step, draw your ground plan, marking any openings or variations in the line of the three walls.

Next, draw your *elevation*, placing the uprights along the lines of your ground plan. Sketch in your doors, windows, fire-place, alcoves, and wall decorations.

As the third step, get a tin color box and brush, such as are used by school children, and sketch in the color scheme. Perhaps you may need to postpone your color work until you have read the chapter on scene painting, but be careful to get effective color combinations, and employ those giving the best emphasis to the nature of the play.

If you have access to a model miniature stage, take its dimensions, and then translate your sketched design into a concrete setting made according to these dimensions. Use plain white cardboard, which can be painted, for your walls and ceiling, cutting out the openings and making the variations in wall lines as indicated in your sketch. In other words, make your set according to your elevation sketch, and paint it according to your colored sketch.

If there is no model stage, one may be made out of a shoe box, or some other box of paper or wood, that is at least twice as wide as it is deep, and that allows for a proscenium opening at least two thirds as high. A good scale to adopt is the professional one of $\frac{1}{2}$ inch to the foot.

Assuming that you are planning a set 18 feet wide, 12 feet deep and 12 feet high, your miniature dimensions will then be, in inches, 9 x 6 for back wall, and 6 x 6 for each side wall. Into these walls, cut your doors and windows, taking care not to make them off scale. If a door is 6 x 2 feet, in round figures, in your model it would be 3 x 1 inches. Windows must be cut at the conventional distance from floor and ceiling. The fireplace, if there is to be one, might come about half way up to the ceiling. You may cut your walls out of a solid sheet of cardboard, or make them out of flats 6 x 3 inches. Three of these will give a back wall 9 inches wide and 6 inches high. Side walls will contain two flats each 6 x 3, or a wall 6 inches high and 6 inches wide. These flats may be fastened together in various ways, but adhesive tape or gum paper are as good a device as any other. When you have your sketch thus transposed into a three dimensional form, make your door and window frames to show *reveal* (see glossary). This will not be hard to do by the aid of a little paste and a pair of scissors. Hinging on the doors may call for some ingenuity.

Now paint the walls, first a solid ground color, then stipple according to the sketch (see *stipple* in glossary). Paint the doors and window frames in pleasing contrast to the walls.

Now your stage is ready for the furniture. Find what you need in a toy shop, or better still, make it out of modeling clay or cardboard. Take care that it is made strictly to scale, neither too large nor too small for the interior, and that it has the line and color in harmony with walls, and with conditions of life represented in the play. Drape your windows in harmonious colors and appropriate lines. Strive always for a life-like and technically correct setting, and judge it by the *artistic* illusion it creates.

QUESTIONS

1. Describe the Greek theatre.
2. What kind of a stage did Shakespeare use?
3. What was the old-fashioned wing set?
4. What is the psychological effect of the *picture frame* element in our modern stage?
5. What is realism, and for what kind of a set does it call?
6. What opportunities does a symbolic play afford the designer?

7. How does the representational method differ from the presentational?
8. What are ground plans, elevations, and color sketches?
9. What is the designer's first step in planning his setting?
10. How can a model stage be of use to amateur producers?

CHAPTER XI

SCENE CONSTRUCTION

A fully equipped theatre is not often available to amateurs. In such case any clear space may be converted into a stage, provided there is also an adequate seating area. As any frank conformity to necessity is acceptable art, a platform may be constructed in the corner of the gymnasium, or other building, to serve as a temporary makeshift.

Any three act play, within the capacity of the ordinary school group, may be produced on a stage with a proscenium opening between 15 and 40 feet in width, and 8 to 15 feet in height. The depth should not be less than 10 feet. Beyond that, the deeper the better. Too much height is cut down by the teaser; too much width by tormentors; the back walls set the limit to excessive depth. These minimum dimensions obviously call for plays of one setting and with small casts.

On an improvised stage, the act curtain is the first consideration, and may be one of three types. The *draw* type opens and closes laterally, the *tableau* type swings out and up diagonally, and the ordinary *drop* rolls up on a spool or is pulled up on pulleys.

For the school stage, with no space above the arch, the draw type is the most satisfactory. Any inexpensive material, which looks and hangs well, is made up in two parts which together cover the proscenium opening. A strong wire is stretched across the opening just a little behind and above the arch.

133

If the material is heavy, an iron rod may be used instead of wire. The curtains slide along this rod, or wire, on rings set into the upper hem of the material at about six inches apart.

The curtains are operated from one side, by means of cords correctly arranged, over a system of pulleys.

A simpler method of arranging the draw curtain is described by Phillip Barber as illustrated in the accompanying sketch, which also adequately describes the tableau type. The drop curtain may be manipulated over pulleys, where height permits, on a spool that winds the curtain up.

The scenery may be either the *hanging* or the *standing* type. In case of the hanging type, wires are stretched across the point of the auditorium, one running parallel to the back wall, and the other two parallel to the side walls. Any light inexpensive material may be hung from these wires to form a hanging *box set*. The extra weight of more expensive velvet would necessitate the use of gas pipe or iron rods instead of wires.

Returning to the *wing* system of other days, an interesting double setting may be achieved. At twelve-inch intervals, wires are stretched across the stage above the arch, and are made taut by turnbuckles. In a stage twelve feet deep, there would be twelve wires running parallel to the back wall. From these, light material in two colors is hung by snap hooks fastened to the upper hem at three-inch intervals. The lengths are cut to floor lengths and the lower hem is weighted so that the curtains will hang properly. It should be understood that the widths of material are not sewn together. They hang better separately, and afford convenient openings at any point desired.

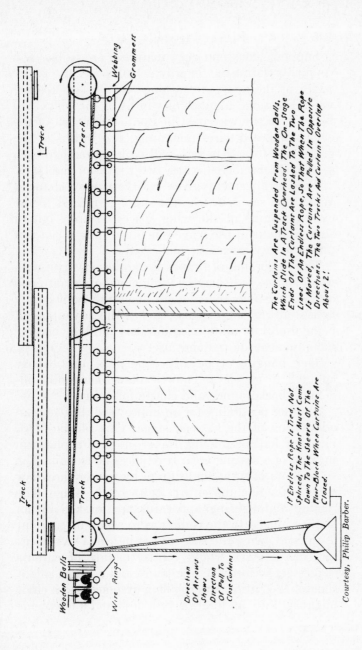

The Curtains Are Suspended From Wooden Balls, Which Slide In A Track Overhead. The On-Stage Ends Of The Curtains Are Lashed To The Two Lines Of An Endless Rope, So That When The Rope Is Moved, The Curtains Are Pulled In Opposite Directions. The Two Tracks And Curtains Overlap About 2'.

If Endless Rope Is Tied, Not Spliced, The Knot Must Come Down To The Sheeve Of The Floor-Block When Curtains Are Closed.

Direction Of Arrows Shows Direction Of Pull To Close Curtains

Courtesy, Philip Barber.

Suppose black and gray materials are to be used. As many widths of the gray as will cover the entire width of the stage are fastened to the last upstage wire. The same number of widths of the black will be hung to the wire next in front. From each of the even numbered wires remaining, two widths of the gray—one to each wing—will be hung, and to each of the odd numbered wires, two widths of the black.

This arrangement gives two very easy changes. When one set is in use, the other is retired to the extreme limits of the wing spaces, entirely out of sight and out of the way. When carefully done, this makes a very attractive makeshift.

The cyclorama of drapes is another favorite with small stages, as it may be hung circularly or at open angles. This may be ordered to measure from supply houses at varying expense. It has the advantage of being useful for all public functions, but may become monotonous if in frequent use.

The hanging type of scenery is particularly adapted to classic and poetic plays demanding indefinite backgrounds and chaste formality.

Another possibility for an improvised theatre is an adaptation of the Copeau stage. This can be fitted into any hall permitting the erection of a platform in front of a seating area. It requires no curtain. The stage flows into the auditorium by two or three low steps extending the entire width of the stage. The rigging and lighting apparatus are masked by an arch so hinged to the ceiling as to swing up and out of the way when the stage is not in use. The scenery for such a stage would consist mainly of cutouts suggesting locality. A tree trunk and a bench might suggest the entire park, while a fireplace and a chair might indicate an interior, or a desk and a telephone

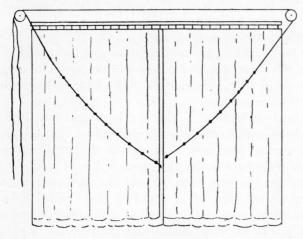

REAR VIEW
CURTAIN CLOSED

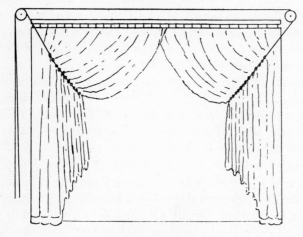

REAR VIEW
CURTAIN OPEN

A "TAB" CURTAIN
Not Drawn To Scale

Courtesy, Philip Barber

an office. If the stage is large enough, all three sets can be placed in position at once, and picked up in turn by the spotlight. Obviously, this does not bring any effect of reality, but it may carry with it the effect of classic art.

The best method is the one best suited to local conditions. It should also be well suited to the style of the play produced. *As You Like It* plays best in a natural grove under the open sky.

By far the best method, and the one used most often, is the box set of standing units called *flats*. This set is easily constructed, at a small initial cost, and it can be inexpensively re-painted and re-arranged to yield new results for a long succession of plays. The flat may be any width necessary to correspond to the width of cloth to be used. This is between one yard and 72 inches. The latter will cover a flat six feet wide, a good width particularly if the flats are not to be shipped by rail.

Seven six-foot flats are adequate for any ordinary setting. Three for the back wall, and two at the sides, give an interior 18 feet wide and 12 feet deep. This will take care of any play in one setting. Another set of flats made in the same way, but painted differently, will provide for plays in two sets. These two sets of seven flats may constitute the original working scenic capital, to which may be added other units as finances permit. Of each set of seven flats, at least two should be door flats and at least one a window flat. These may be so constructed as to be easily convertible into a solid flat by sealing the opening with a piece to fit. An archway may be an extra flat, or a piece fitted between two regular flats. Irregularities in the walls may be made with jogs, or extra narrow flats painted in harmony with the sets and kept for emergencies.

To Construct a Flat Setting.—First decide upon the height of the set. Professional stages use flats 18 feet or more in height. For the small stage 12 feet is high enough. Plan to make two sets of seven flats 12 feet high and six feet wide, or fourteen flats in all.

From the lumber yard order:

White pine lumber, 1 x 2, for the flat frames, enough to give twenty-eight *stiles*, the same number of *battens*, and the same of toggle-bars, with additional lumber for bracing.

White pine, 1 x 4, or 1 x 6, for door and window frames and facings.

A supply of three-ply veneer for *corner-blocks* and *keystones*.

From the drygoods store, get canvas, or preferably the cheaper unbleached muslin, in the 72-inch width. You will need a twenty-eight yard bolt for each of the seven flat sets.

At the hardware buy:

Clout nails, 1¼ inch.

Carpet tacks, screw eyes, screws of various lengths, nails.

Hinges, putty, lash line, lash cleats, brace hooks and eyes, and other articles that may suggest themselves as you proceed.

In the tool chest should be:

A hammer; two or three saws—rip, cross and band; squares; rules; planes; brace and bits; chisels; a clinching iron; a mitre-box; marking pencils.

Cut the lumber all at one time, making the twenty-eight stiles of exactly the same length. There must not be a quarter of an inch variation, or the flats will not stand square. These lengths will be

12 feet minus 4 inches, the four inches being made up by the two-inch battens at top and bottom. Cut twenty-eight six-foot lengths for the battens, and twenty-eight pieces six feet minus four inches, the four inches being taken up by the two stiles between which your cross pieces are fitted.

In order to make the squaring of the corners more accurate, you fasten to the floor timbers to form a perfect square, or square *form*, six feet wide. Against the cross piece of the form you lay your batten, and along the other side of the right angle you lay your stile. One stile and batten being thus squared, the pieces opposite will automatically form a rectangle.

Having cut the three-ply into corner-blocks and keystones, place the clinching iron under each corner in turn, and fasten the corner blocks with clout nails. Thus the ends of the stiles and battens are firmly joined together. This makes all mitre work, and all dove-tailing unnecessary. No other nails are driven into the wood.

After fastening the four corners to make perfect right angles, strengthen the frames by clouting the toggle-bars to the stiles by means of the keystone. To provide for strength and rigidity, cut extra pieces of the lumber in your mitre-box, and clout them to the corners by way of angle braces. The battens overlap the stiles to prevent the ends from chipping as the flats are slid along the floor.

The door flat is made like the others, except that a frame is provided for the opening in the lower part. This usually is 6'6" high and 2'10" wide. Place two extra stiles 6½ feet long between the bottom batten, and a toggle-bar 6½ feet above, using corner blocks and keystones as before. Then cut out the portion of the lower batten between the two stiles and replace

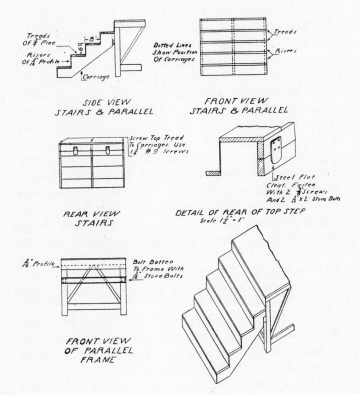

Treads
Of ¾" Pine

Risers
Of ⅜" Profile →

8"

6¼"

Carriage

SIDE VIEW
STAIRS & PARALLEL

Dotted Lines
Show Position
Of Carriages

Treads

Risers

FRONT VIEW
STAIRS & PARALLEL

Screw Top Tread
To Carriages. Use
1¼" #9 Screws

REAR VIEW
STAIRS

Steel Flat
Cleat. Fasten
With 2 ⅝" Screws
And 2 ¼" X 2" Store Bolts

DETAIL OF REAR OF TOP STEP
Scale 1½" = 1'

⅜" Profile

Bolt Batten
To Frame With
⅜" Stove Bolts

FRONT VIEW
OF PARALLEL
FRAME

ISOMETRIC PERSPECTIVE

STRAIGHT-RUN STAIRS
Scale ½" = 1'

Courtesy, Philip Barber

it with a sill iron, which may be made to order at a tin shop. The window flat is made the same as the door flat, except that the opening is not carried to the floor, but is cut off by an extra toggle-bar.

When the flats are constructed, you turn them one by one smooth face up and lay the canvas. Lay your cloth flush with the sides. Tack it first along one stile, putting the tacks at four-inch intervals one-fourth of an inch from the *inner* edge of the frame. Then tack the same way along one of the battens. For the rest alternate between the other stile and batten, taking care that the canvas lies smooth, but *not tight*. The sizing with glue will stretch the cloth to the desired tension, as well as fasten the edges to the wood. Cover the door and window flats as any others, waiting until they have been painted to cut the openings. Then this painted piece can be stretched on a frame and used to seal the opening when a solid flat is needed.

If you want a ceiling for the set, it can be made on the principle of a quilting frame. Attach the cloth to two battens slightly longer than the entire width of the stage. Then the width of the cloth between these battens will correspond to the depth of the set. Fasten these two battens to two others hung parallel to the side walls of the set. Pin or bolt the ends together like the pieces of the quilting frame. These side battens may be permanently fastened in place, or hung so as to be removable. When not in use, the canvas is rolled up for storage.

The book-type ceiling consists of two flats which, hinged together, cover the entire space, and fold more conveniently for storage. When the box set first came into use, the doors and windows were very simple openings in the canvas. The facings were painted on. Now real door and window frames are used, showing *reveal,* or thickness of the wall.

For these frames and facings use 1 x 4, or 1 x 6 inch stuff, according to the width of wall or facing desired. The frames are simply constructed in two parts, one representing the reveal, the other the facing. These are fastened together. The frame must be small enough to fit quite *loosely* into the opening. The facing will keep it from slipping out backward, and a set of gate-hinges fastened at an angle on the outside of the frame will clamp it to the flat to prevent its slipping forward. These frames may be nailed together end to end. Or they may be elaborately fitted with any of the various types of joint known to the trade. A sill for the window and a tread for the door are easily fitted.

The process of construction is now finished. Fasten the eye screws into the upper inner corners of the flats, and a system of lash cleats along the inner edges of the stiles, with a tie-off cleat at the lower end. These cleats may be ordered at the supply house, or made to order at the tin shop. Any rigid piece of steel that can be screwed to the wood to project over the inner edge of the stile will do.

The flats may be joined together in pairs by pin-hinges to facilitate setting up. If back stage space permits, the flats may be fitted with eyes for the professional brace hooks, or may be provided with jacks hinged to the back to open like the gate-leg of a table.

It should be clearly understood that this method of constructing scenery is better adapted to amateur use than to professional. The college theatre is usually stationary. The scenery is not often transported in box cars, or subjected to other rough usage.

It does not need the expensive material and the elaborate workmanship that must go into the professional set, which must be constructed to withstand all kinds of rough handling on the road.

Instead of the *butt* joint suggested here, the professional scene builder may prefer to use the *mitre* joint, *halved* joint, *notched* joint, or the open or closed *mortise and tenon* joint. These he reinforces with glue. He selects his wood carefully. His batten timber must be long, light, straight, and flawless. The ordinary lumber yard cannot afford to carry such pieces, and the college amateur could not afford to purchase it. The method described will be found satisfactory for amateur use, if the flats are constructed in a workmanlike manner.

Assignments

1. Using a cigar box, or something similar; small pulleys, or ring substitutes; light cord; any kind of cloth: arrange a curtain of the draw type across the opening of your box.

2. Draw sketches of: a plain flat, on the canvas side, showing position of tacks; a window or a door flat on the back side, showing keystones, corner-blocks, toggle-bars, braces, stiles, battens, and the extra pieces needed for the opening.

3. From your sketches, select one of the flats. Using thin pieces of wood, nails or tacks in proportion, and canvas, carefully construct a miniature flat, to scale, for your model stage. This can be used later for an experiment in scene painting.

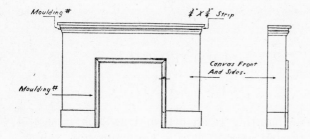

Moulding #

¾" X ¾" Strip

Moulding #

Canvas Front
And Sides.

FRONT VIEW
FIRE PLACE

SIDE VIEW

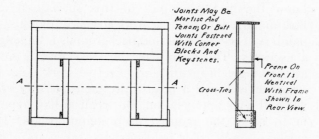

Joints May Be
Mortise And
Tenon; Or Butt
Joints Fastened
With Corner
Blocks And
Keystones.

A   A

Frame On
Front Is
Identical
With Frame
Shown In
Rear View.

Cross-Ties

REAR VIEW
Mantel And Moulding Removed

SIDE VIEW
Moulding And Canvas
Removed

SECTION A-A

The Two Frames Are
Built Separately. They
Are Assembled With
The Four Cross-Ties, And
The Mantel And Base Trim
Nailed Into Place. The Canvas
Is Tacked And Glued Into
Place, And The Moulding
Nailed On.

A FIREPLACE
Scale ½" = 1'

Courtesy, Philip Barber

CHAPTER XII

SCENE PAINTING

Scene painting is an art, and as such it should be entrusted only to artists. Unfortunately, the art departments of colleges frequently do not care to undertake scene painting, and, more often, do not know the first principles of this specialized art. Fortunately, the exacting work formerly required of painters of scenic drops and backgrounds is no longer a necessity. The history of the stage reveals some astonishingly beautiful and effective work done by scenic artists, and a beautifully done piece of canvas still wins appreciation. But realism has stepped in to make the painted drop inappropriate. The cyclorama and color lighting have taken its place.

The main problem for the college amateur is to get his plastic pieces painted with the objectives of good taste and effective projection. Such work can be done fairly well by anyone who has an eye for color and can wield a brush.

For this reason this chapter will need to be little more than a formula. As such it will serve as a basis for enjoyable and valuable experiments in the laboratory.

The flats are now ready for sizing and painting. Fourteen flats will call for about four pounds of flake glue, a supply of whiting in bulk or package, powdered pigment in the colors to be used singly or in combination, paint brushes ranging in size from a large white-wash brush to fine liners, a yardstick for short lines and a 12-foot batten for drawing lines across wider distances, a large sponge for stipple work, and some cloths for various purposes. In addition to this material you will need a heater of some kind. A small electric grill is perhaps the most satisfactory.

The first step is to *size* the canvas. Let the glue soak overnight in a pail of cold water. In the morning cook the resulting jelly, stirring constantly to prevent scorching. When the glue is completely liquefied, add whiting powder and water enough to get six pailfuls of mixture, which should cover the entire job. Use enough of the whiting to make the mixture the consistency of heavy cream. Put the whiting in while the glue is still hot, and keep stirring to avoid lumps.

There are several convenient ways of arranging the flats for painting. They may be hung horizontally along the wall about waist high, or laid on horses about the same height. The third way is to lay them on the floor. This method is hard unless the painter uses a long handled brush. The wall method, where practicable, is the best, as all parts of the six-foot flat are easily reached from the floor, or from a low scaffold or stool.

In the professional theatre the painter has a paint-bridge up in the gridiron where he can work without being disturbed. His flats are elevated into the proper position by ropes and pulleys.

First apply the size mixture, spreading it thickly and evenly over the entire surface, taking care to paste down the loose edges of the canvas to the stiles and battens. This process tenses the canvas, fills in the pores of the mesh, and glues the cloth to the wood. If the process has been followed according to specifications, the face of the flat will be firm, smooth and opaque. If the size mixture had too much glue, the canvas will have a tendency to crack. If not enough glue has been used, the cloth will be transparent. Too much powder in the sizing mixture makes the brushing heavy; too little makes the coat thin.

As soon as this coat is dry, the flat is ready for the laying-in process. In a rush job this process may be combined with the sizing by the use of pigment powder in place of the whiting. This gives the size and the ground color at the same time, and saves the laying-in operation. The mixture containing the glue must be kept warm to prevent the glue from congealing, and it must be frequently stirred to keep the powder from settling.

While the size coat is drying, study the color scheme. The pigment primaries are red, yellow, and blue. Any variety of secondary colors may be formed from these by mixing in given proportions. Orange, for instance, is the result of red and yellow mixed in equal parts, and half way between red and orange is orange-red. Yellow and blue makes green; blue and red gives violet.

You should have a color wheel in mind, or on a chart, at least until thoroughly familiar with color derivation.

With a compass describe a circle. Divide it into six segments, marking each segment a color, red, orange, yellow, green, blue, violet. Within this larger circle, draw a small one at the center and mark it gray. This will give a simple color-wheel with which to work out the following details:

Analogous colors are those adjacent on the wheel, such as red and orange.

Complementaries are those opposite, such as red and green.

Any two complementaries mixed in equal parts make gray.

Hue is the true value of color.

Intensity depends upon the amount of the complement in the mixture.

Value depends upon the amount of white or black admixture.

A *shade* is the color with black predominant.

A *tint* is color with predominating white.

A clash is produced by two colors approximately 90 degrees apart on the wheel.

Yellow contains the most light of all the colors.

No color surpasses red for effectiveness on the stage.

Red, orange, yellow and their derivatives are the *warm* colors.

Green, blue, violet and derivatives are the *cool* colors.

The cool colors nature uses in wild profusion are not so striking on the stage as the warm ones nature uses sparingly.

Any colors are harmonious if mixed in the right proportion.

Lighter tints are more stimulating; darker shades are more dignified.

A small amount of light color overcomes much gray.

Shades and tints of the same color may be mixed in any proportion.

Analogous hues may be mixed in any proportion, if no other colors are added.

Complementary colors may be mixed in any proportion.

Light tints and shades may, if in the same class, be mixed with neutrals in any proportion.

Intense colors may be mixed with neutrals in any proportion. On a large surface the neutrals should predominate.

A neutral background may be used to *tie* colors that would clash if placed close together.

Whiting may be used to secure lighter tones of any color, but too much whiting robs the color of brilliance.

Mixing colors is the one problem in scene painting. The brush work is so simple that it can be delegated to any intelligent and careful assistant. As exact blends are practically impossible to duplicate, except by happy accident, prepare enough mixture in one process and in one container to cover the entire job. Never forget that the wet mixture is always several shades darker than the dry final result. To test it, dab a thin coat on a slab where it will dry quickly, and where the effect can be judged in a few minutes.

By the time the colors are mixed, the prime coat is dry. The mixture for this second coat must not be too warm, or it will smear the prime coat. Six gallons should cover one set of seven flats. The same amount of another ground coat should take care of the other set. This laying-in process is done by spreading the mixture evenly with a small brush.

You may be satisfied with this coat, a plain surface of one solid color. But if a richer effect is preferred, some stipple work is necessary. Suppose the upper one-third of the flat is to be this solid color. Then draw a ribbon an inch wide of some harmoniously contrasting color, using the long batten as a guide to give a straight and continuous line along the whole of the three walls of the set. If the color scheme is a combination of red and yellow, a strip of gold makes an effective line of demarcation between the two sections of the flat.

Below this line apply the stipple. Cut a sponge in half to get a level face, and prepare a mixture brighter than the ground hue. Dip the sponge into it lightly, and carefully dab it on the ground coat. This results in an interesting design corresponding to the irregular, yet constant, pattern of the sponge. Being careful not to smear, gives you a uniform pattern of broken color, as delicate and intricate as the pores of the sponge. This, under artificial light, will blend with the ground color to form a richer surface than the ground color alone. Thus several harmonious colors may be superimposed, each of which may be emphasized in turn by means of colored lighting. It is understood that clashing hues cannot be used in this work.

Stipple work may be done in several other ways, each of which will bring its own design or pattern. It may be done by *rolling,* which requires a rag rolled up as if being wrung dry to be dipped in paint, and touched to the surface of the flat. It may be done by *spattering,* which means dipping the brush in paint, and striking it over the wrist, dashing the paint in a sort of spray design. Another method is *scumbling,* or dipping the brush lightly and spreading the paint very thinly over the ground color in fine streaks. Stipple, or broken color, or *pointillism,* as it is variously called, is the result of a solid background of color with one or more harmonious hues sponged, rolled, spattered, or scumbled over it.

Stucco may be suggested by applying in much the same way more widely separate colors.

Old stained surfaces may be suggested by scumbling on spots of browns, reds, yellows, or blues.

Variety and unusual lighting effects may be had by painting into the walls at the natural places shades and tones of the color.

Brick walls are more convincing when painted in the natural irregularity of design.

Rough boards may be imitated with dark brown ground color, the outlines drawn in charcoal, and the proper shades scumbled over in irregularly parallel strokes to represent the grain of the timbers. Any kind of graining effect is achieved with yellow ochre mixed with whiting, and scumbled on in bold strokes of an almost dry brush. The rough grain of a log cabin may be suggested by pasting on wrinkled cloth, and scumbling over it horizontally. As logs run the full length of the wall, the painted mortar lines must be unbroken across all the flats composing the wall. Dark grays, browns, or blues are the best colors to scumble over the entire surface.

A break in the canvas may be repaired by pasting an irregular edged piece of cloth over the hole, painting it with the color of the flat. A rip may be repaired by using gummed paper.

With the flats done, the next step is painting the door and window frames and facings. Oil paints should be used for greater durability, but powdered pigment will do. It has the double advantage of being cheaper and of drying more quickly. It can also be quickly changed from one color to another.

Next take care of the backing for the doors and windows. These may be simple screens for each separate opening, a general sky dome, or an extra flat painted to represent a hallway or terrace. If

the stage is equipped with a painted canvas backdrop, and if the painting gives the required background, it may then serve for backing.

The sky dome must be large enough to conceal
the entire backstage space from the audience.
Whether made of canvas or of plaster, it is to be
painted sky color. In a pail of water, mix three or
four ounces of Italian Blue, and apply the mixture
with a large, clean brush. Since the natural sky is
lighter blue near the zenith than at the horizon
line, make the mixture lighter at the beginning
and paint from the top, brushing horizontally along
the entire surface. Keep adding blue powder as you
work downward. In this manner you not only get
a deeper blue toward the horizon line, but also prevent splotching.

Any plastic piece necessary for an exterior setting must now be made. In this connection note that
there are no vast areas of unrelieved color in nature, but rather a constant variety of intermingling
hues. A simple tree trunk may show many analogous
and contrasting colors, as also may a weather-beaten
rock. A distant mountain range displays a mixture
of green, blue, purple, streaked with violet, and
topped with white to represent snow-capped peaks.
All these under ordinary atmospheric conditions
would be light tints.

In representing foliage, you cannot hope to reproduce each individual leaf. Be satisfied with solid
masses of color. Hint at clumps of leaves rather than
at individual patterns. Vines and bushes are best
rented, or purchased from a supply house, or secured
from a local window trimmer.

For mist, or an effect of distance, use scrim, or
dark blue theatrical gauze. If this is lighted from the

rear, it becomes invisible to the audience. When lighted at a slant, the mist effect is intensified without exposing the gauze to view.

It is to be constantly remembered that pigment colors undergo slight changes under colored light. You must be thoroughly familiar with the effect of light primaries on color primaries. This will be discussed in the following chapter.

ASSIGNMENTS

If a new set of scenery is needed for a forthcoming production, use this opportunity to gain actual experience in scene painting. If this is not feasible, work with a miniature stage.

1. Get a section of cardboard, composition board, or some other practical plain surface; or use your model flat constructed previously. From the stock of powder pigments, select the proper hues, mixing them to get the exact effect desired. With a small brush paint the surface with ground color. With sponge, rolled cloth, or with the spatter or other process, stipple over the ground color. In an effectively contrasting hue, work in the baseboard, facings, patterns, or any other decorative effect you would like the interior to show.

2. Those who are particularly interested in the subject should supplement this chapter by studying one or both of the following references:

Scenewright by Andre Smith, Chapter X, Macmillan.
Scenery by Harold Helvensten, pp. 51-60, Stanford Univ. Press.

CHAPTER XIII

STAGE LIGHTING

Stage lighting has an interesting history. The stage in ancient Greece knew only sunlight. Shakespeare's early plays were similarly produced under the foggier light of a London afternoon, but toward the end of his career, Shakespeare had the questionable advantage of candle light.

From the candle, through oil, kerosene, acetylene, and other dangerous media, to electricity was a slow but steady progress. Today the electric bulb seems to be the final answer to the producer's prayer. It is not, perhaps, at the acme of its potentialities, but it seems unalterable in principle. It is hard to imagine any future lighting system that will not make use of electricity in some form. It is easily conceivable, however, that engineers will continue to improve upon the present lighting devices.

There is a vital factor in lighting, second only to the actor in holding the attention of an audience. Our picture frame stage induces a partial hypnosis in the spectator making him more credulous, more easily forgetful of practical realities, and more ready to enter into the spirit of make-believe. This is especially true when the light takes on all the colors of the spectrum, each with power to create its own mood and its own atmosphere.

Every student of the theatre should acquaint himself with some of the systems of lighting that have been employed in modern times. The past has known

155

only one system. Whether candle, kerosene, gas, or electricity, the light was thrown on the stage directly by reflectors. This is known as the direct system of lighting. Footlights and borderlights are survivors of this system. Most theatres still retain the footlights, greatly improved, and the borderlights, or their spot or strip equivalents. In addition to these fixed units, we have all kinds of movable devices. Most of these are members of the direct lighting company, variously improved for increased effectiveness.

One radical departure from the direct lighting system was the so-called Fortuni system of indirect lighting which takes its name from the originator, Mariano Fortuni of Venice. After long experimentation in connection with the German General Electric Company, Fortuni discovered what he thought approximated the diffused light of day. Instead of the direct rays of the old system, he shed a volume of light on the stage indirectly by double reflection. One set of reflectors threw the light away from the stage against another set, which threw it back on the stage in diffused form. To get the desired intensity, he used arc lights. By training these on colored surfaces of silk, he added color to his illumination. This system was found to be most effective on exterior settings. To get the best values, Fortuni invented the skydome against which he could use his system with good effect. This idea has survived in the several types of cyclorama now in use, but it responds just as well to the old direct lighting principle in connection with the color media.

A number of the 1910 *Scientific American* describes the Fortuni system in detail as it was understood at the time of its invention. This system was too ex-

From *Idiot's Delight.*

pensive to remain in use, but it has been very helpful in showing better ways of employing the direct system. The same effect is achieved by sending the light directly through colored gelatine, an invention possibly suggested by the colored silk used by Fortuni.

In his Art Theatre in Berlin, Max Reinhardt adopted indirect lighting as an experiment in *intimacy,* of bringing house and stage closer together. At one time, he had ten thousand bulbs shedding diffused light through walls of silk lining the stage and auditorium alike. In this way he attempted to eliminate the peep show nature of the stage. His experiment was not valuable enough to deserve general adoption.

In connection with color lighting came the companion method of broken color painting. It was the Russian lad, Nicholas DeLipsky, experimenting with camouflage in the war, who first succeeded in painting a set in three superimposed colors, and then bringing each color out separately by means of color in light.

David Belasco was the one genius of the theatre who seemed to be in possession of all the secrets of the art of production. It is even hinted that he had experimented with, and discarded as impracticable, the indirect lighting system before Fortuni announced it. Those who saw his original production of *The Girl Of The Golden West,* early in the present century, before color lighting was generally employed, still recall the unbelievable beauty of some of the settings.

Several attempts besides Reinhardt's have been made to abolish the picture-frame technique of the theatre. So far, all have failed because the light behind the proscenium opening is as alive as the actors themselves. The beauty and the power of this restricted picture are enhanced every time a new color combination is thrown upon it.

Electricity.—Every student of play production should have a general practical knowledge of the terms and principles of electricity.

Voltage means the electro-motive force, or power of the generator.

Volt is the unit of measure of that force.

Current is the rate of flow of the force.

Ampere is the unit of measure of the flow.

Ohm is the unit of resistance to the flow.

A copper wire offers the least resistance to the current. This makes it the best conductor of electricity in use.

Substances offering the most resistance are:

Porcelain, used for sockets and attachments.

Fibre, used in plugs.

Rubber and cotton fabric, used for insulating wires.

The copper wire may carry an ampere of current through a resistance of one ohm with the pressure of one volt.

Watt is the commercial name for the product of volt multiplied by ampere.

The *rheostat,* or *dimmer,* is a device for increasing the resistance to the flow of the current, thereby reducing the intensity of the light.

Light is the general name for the phenomenon.

Illumination designates the particular devices used in lighting.

Lighting is a term applied to the art of producing light effects on the stage.

General illumination lights the actor and his environment, reduces contrasts, and suggests the natural light of day.

Specific illumination may have for its objects:

To relieve eye strain

To beautify the scene

To induce mood

To create atmosphere

To focus attention

To imitate color in nature—sunset, moonlight, dawn.

The main purpose of light, visibility, has found its complement in an important secondary purpose, effect.

"Light is no more the mere possibility of seeing than music is of hearing," says Adolphe Appia.

The shape of the reflector determines what is to become of the light generated by the lamp.

A semi-spherical reflector focuses the rays, as in the spot-light.

A parabolic reflector sends the rays in parallel lines, as in footlights and borderlights.

The lens, or glass through which light passes, refracts the rays. A lens with parallel faces sends them out straight. A concave lens concentrates them. A convex lens spreads them out.

The light bulbs in use now are of two types: the pear-shaped, and the globular. The pear-shaped bulb burns without damage in any position, and has a life of about 1,000 hours. The globular bulb has a life of only two hundred hours. It expires quickly if burned base up.

Globular lamps are made in two strengths: the small base of 500 watts; and the mogul base of 1,000 watts. Higher wattage lamps are made for a limited market.

An object is visible because it reflects light shed upon it.

Substances upon which light falls are translucent, opaque, or transparent.

No substance known gives 100% reflection. White surfaces come nearest with 95%. We wear white in hot seasons for a better reason than attractiveness. Black reflects the smallest amount of light with a bare .004%. Other colors come anywhere between the two extremes.

Reflection is of four types:

Regular, as in a mirror

Diffuse, as in daylight

Spread, differing from diffuse by the angle of incidence which prevents complete diffusion

Specular, a combination of regular and diffuse.

The question then becomes: what kind of reflection will give the desired effect, and of what material shall the reflecting surface be?

Any recent catalogue of a good electric company carries a clear description of all the devices employed up to date. Experiments are going on constantly, and tomorrow may find any statement in today's book obsolete.

The following list of devices may suggest the opportunity the modern electrician has for producing varied lighting effects:

Footlights, arranged in open troughs, or in separate compartments for each bulb.

Borderlights, of the same two types.

Proscenium lights, of the same two types.

Open-box floodlights, with or without standards, or hangers.

Spots of all powers, suspended or on standards.

Bunch lights, a cluster of bulbs variously applied.

Strip lights, a row of bulbs in a portable reflecting trough, to be used horizontally or vertically on any part of the stage.

Olivettes, square, open boxes with powerful bulbs, on adjustable standards, for throwing light from behind the scene.

The most recent improvement, perhaps, is the enclosing of each bulb of the foot- and borderlights in separate reflecting chambers fitted with a slot for the color frame. This does away with the colored glass bulb, which was never permanently satisfactory. It also prevents the colored rays from mingling at the source, as they do in the open trough reflector.

The most marked improvement has come in the dimmer, and with the invention of the color medium. The electric switch throws the light on and off abruptly; the dimmer graduates the intensity from full illumination to a complete fade-out. The gelatine clothes the scene with color. It is inexpensive, effective, and easily applied.

This medium is made in large square sheets, which may be used in their entirety in large box reflectors, or cut up into smaller sections to fit smaller lamps.

The Rosco Laboratories announce the following colors in gelatine:

Red—medium, fire, light.

Orange—dark amber, amber, medium amber, light amber.

Yellow—pale amber, straw, dark lemon, medium lemon, no color straw.

Green—medium, dark, light, blue-green, green-blue (Moonlight).

Blue—urban, dark, medium, sky, light, special
  steel, daylight.

Purple—dark, medium, light, rose, deep pink,
  non-fading pink, dark and medium lavender,
  surprise pink, dark, medium and light magen-
  tas, deep flesh, flesh pink, no color pink, frost.

Specials—neutral gray, smoke, special light
  amber, flame tint, chocolate, violet, yellow-
  green, rainbow colors.

In using these media, remember that light color
has a tendency to wash out pigment color. Pigment
primaries are red, yellow, and blue. Light primaries
are red, green, and violet.

In general, a given color in light tends to wash
out the same color in costume, wall, or furniture.

The Rosco Laboratories, after careful experimenting, name the following results:

Red	light on	Red	surface yields		Gray
Red	"	" Orange	"	"	Red-Red-Gray
Red	"	" Yellow	"	"	Red-Red-Gray
Red	"	" Green	"	"	Brown or Gray
Red	"	" Blue	"	"	Black
Red	"	" Violet	"	"	Red-Gray
Red	"	" Brown	"	"	Gray-Brown
Yellow	"	" Red	"	"	Red
Yellow	"	" Orange	"	"	Orange
Yellow	"	" Yellow	"	"	Yellow
Yellow	"	" Green	"	"	Green
Yellow	"	" Blue	"	"	Blue
Yellow	"	" Violet	"	"	Violet
Yellow	"	" Brown	"	"	Brown
Green	"	" Red	"	"	Dark-red or black
Green	"	" Orange	"	"	Dark-orange
Green	"	" Yellow	"	"	Yellow
Green	"	" Green	"	"	Gray
Green	"	" Blue	"	"	Dark-blue

Green	light on	Violet	surface yields	Blue-gray
Green	" "	Brown	" "	Brown to black
Blue	" "	Red	"	"	Dark-red
Blue	" "	Orange	"	"	Light-orange
Blue	" "	Yellow	"	"	Yellow-orange
Blue	" "	Green	"	"	Light-blue or gray
Blue	" "	Blue	"	"	Blue-gray
Blue	" "	Violet	"	"	Lavender
Blue	" "	Brown	"	"	Red-brown to black

From this table, which may be misleading in some respects, it is seen that yellow is the most friendly light.

The table also warns that a setting may be changed by means of color lighting, either for better or worse.

It is to be remembered always that colored light is not to be used for its own sake. It is to be reserved for special natural or psychological effects.

ASSIGNMENTS

1. List all the books on lighting available in the library.

2. Make a list of all the most useful types of lighting device advertised in first class supply houses.

3. Borrow from the laboratory a piece of gelatine, and with the aid of focused light find the effect of the color on fabric of various colors.

4. You have now made a sketch design, a miniature set for the model stage, and have painted this set. Train a spotlight on the whole and see how it will look under various colors. Select the effect you like best.

CHAPTER XIV

STAGE SETTING

Stage setting is so closely related to designing that the two may seem to cover the same ground. In designing, however, we were mainly concerned with preliminary plans. Now we are to carry out those plans on the stage.

The first step is to assemble the furniture to be used in a group toward the front of the stage, where it will be out of the way for the present. This will be properly distributed after the flats are set up.

The next step is to put up the set. This task may be simplified in either of two ways: two flats may be pin-hinged together to form the corner of the interior. Opened at an angle, they will stand firmly without bracing, and the other flats may be lashed to them. Or, the flats forming one wall may be laid face down together, fastened together with a long batten at top and bottom, and then raised as a unit and lashed together at the corners.

The first method enables one man to set the stage without much difficulty; the second calls for a crew of several men. The second method insures better alignment for flats, but it is too cumbersome to be useful where wing space is limited.

Lashing a flat is an art in itself. The novice may find it necessary to spend considerable time in the attempt, and at last may have to turn it over to an expert. A little practice will make him skillful.

The walls must not only look solid, but must

actually be firm. If the opening or the shutting of a door makes them wobble, the confidence of the audience wavers with them.

The professional way to avoid this is by the use of the stage brace. This can be used only where back stage space is adequate, and if the floor need not be protected. The floor screw makes a noticeable hole, which would too seriously injure a hardwood floor.

Another way is by the use of jacks, hinged to the flat and weighted down to the floor with sandbags.

A third way, not very convenient, is to fasten a batten to the frame of the flat, and nail the other end of it to some solid surface.

It is understood that the flats will occupy the position indicated by the requirements of the action; the arch, door and windows being placed according to specifications.

In planning the positions of doors and windows, the principles of balance and utility must be observed. Many opportunities for balance with variety will suggest themselves to the artistic eye, but there must be more than balance. Since the openings are to be used by actors in their movements on and off the stage, they must be placed for effective use.

Center back makes the most effective entrance, and is the best place for the most frequently used entrance. Effective, though less emphatic, entrances may be arranged in either side wall as the demands of the action suggest. The important point is to have the side walls open generously toward the audience, so that any opening or important decoration will be clearly visible from any part of the house.

Provide just enough entrances to meet the de-

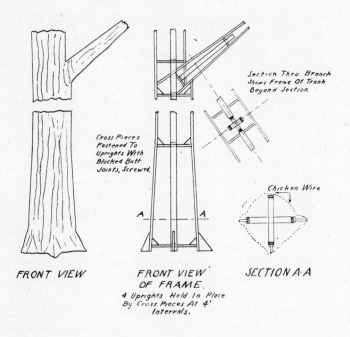

Section Thru Branch
Shows Frame Of Trunk
Beyond Section.

Cross Pieces
Fastened To
Uprights With
Blocked Butt
Joints, Screwed.

Chicken Wire

A   A

FRONT VIEW

FRONT VIEW
OF FRAME.
4 Uprights Held In Place
By Cross Pieces At 4'
Intervals.

SECTION A·A

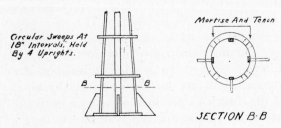

Circular Sweeps At
18" Intervals, Held
By 4 Uprights.

Mortise And Tenon

B   B

SECTION B·B

FRONT·VIEW·OF·FRAME

A TREE TRUNK
Scale ½" = 1'

Courtesy, Philip Barber

mands of the play. A door leads the audience to expect that someone will open it sooner or later. This makes a dummy door a waste of attention. If the set has an extra unnecessary door flat, it may be converted into a window flat and used for balance.

Hinge the doors so that they will open up stage and out. Hung thus they leave the stage free for action, and serve as effectual masking when the door is open.

Arrange the tormentors and all masking pieces to hide all back stage space from the eyes of the audience.

The walls, both in decoration and arrangement, should be true to the locale, and to the spirit of the play. They must not attract undue attention because of either inappropriate luxuriousness, or conspicuous inadequacy.

The picture must acquaint the audience at a glance with the time, the place, and the nature of the action. It should also hint at the social and economic status, taste, race, nationality, and culture of the folk that occupy the environment.

Having set up the flats, next arrange the furniture. There are no more rigid rules for furnishing a stage interior than there are for furnishing any actual interior. Both are largely governed by good taste. But the director's problem is entirely different from that of the home-maker. The stage interior must be seen by the audience from one point of view only, and, from this point of view, it must be seen to the best advantage. This gives us a good working principle. All elements are to be arranged with reference to the audience. During the vogue of extreme realism in stage settings, this was too often disregarded with decidedly bad effect.

Since the audience is to be considered first, last, and always, we may adopt a fundamental law, which will govern the arrangement of furniture now, as well as the relative positions of the actors later. The law is this:

With the center of the auditorium as the pivot point, and with the center of the stage as the other point of a compass, describe an arc of a circle. This arc will run from downstage right to upstage center and to downstage left. All the points on this segment of the circle will be equidistant from the center of the auditorium, and all straight lines from all points on this arc will converge there.

To get the most effective distribution of furniture, follow loosely this curved line. But take care not to obstruct the entrance, or clutter up the acting spaces. Aside from this precaution, place the pieces most used in the business in the most emphatic positions.

Attention naturally focuses on the magnetic center of the picture, which is usually a little to the left of the mathematical center. Following the arc line, place the most important pieces, a table and two chairs, upstage center. Downstage right, may be a writing desk and small chair, and downstage left a sofa for balance and utility. Purely ornamental, or little used articles should be placed according to balance, good taste, and the illusion of reality.

Arranged on this plan, the setting will open toward the audience, and the actors who occupy such acting orbits will approximate facing the audience.

Geometric precision in following this principle is to be avoided. A sort of careless balance is more convincing on the stage than studied perfection.

Furniture is not to imitate, but merely to suggest

reality. The type of home the play depicts may be projected most effectively by a few well chosen pieces. Crowding the stage with multiplicity of detail is comparatively ineffective. The placing of the pieces, too, should only suggest actual arrangement. For example, you cannot place the sofa on the stage as you saw it standing so tastefully in your friend's home. You must be governed by the requirements of action, with respect to the spectator placed in a very definitely fixed position. Your friend had to consult her taste and preference only.

Guard against crowding the acting areas. Good taste must conspire with good judgment to preserve balance on the one hand, and to provide for the effective interpretation of the play on the other. Use no odd piece of furniture that would attract too much attention, unless such concentration is a point in the play.

In planning a setting, always respect the author's picture, but feel free to modify it to suit local conditions. If this can be done without doing violence to the spirit of the play, no author will seriously object.

Conventions in stage setting are as changeable as styles in acting, or customs in dress and demeanor. The Greek audience expected, and got, nothing more than an occasional altar for sacrifice. Shakespeare's audiences were quite well satisfied with a predominantly auditory impression, although we are told that magnificent settings were in vogue elsewhere long before his time. Chinese settings have always remained ridiculously (to us) childlike in their naïve simplicity.

Our own age has adopted, and, in turn, rejected many styles in setting, ranging from the most faith-

Set for *Nice People* designed by local stock company artist.

ful imitation of actuality to the extreme of Shakespearean simplicity.

The best way is to steer some carefully surveyed middle course.

ASSIGNMENTS

Read a play, carefully noting the author's specifications for setting. Then draw a ground plan for openings, furniture, stairway, balcony, etc., planning for good balance, good arrangement with respect to the audience, and ample provision for acting space.

Read another play, or use the same if time is limited, and draw an elevation, sketching in pictures on the wall, draperies, ornaments of all kinds.

Read a play, note the requirements of the setting, and then set the practice stage as nearly as facilities will permit. Be careful to make it both practical and artistic.

CHAPTER XV

MAKE-UP

Make-up in some form has always been practiced by both men and women, both on the stage and off. Among primitive peoples it was studiedly grotesque and exaggerated to frighten enemies. In civilized society it has been used to attract, rather than to repel.

Street make-up has always been in vogue, but perhaps never so universally used by women of all classes as at present. Make-up seems to have become a social necessity.

Reference to the *vice* of make-up are frequent in Shakespeare's works, and in those of other writers of the past. Hamlet exclaims over Yorick's skull: "Now get you to my lady's chamber and tell her, let her paint an inch thick, to this favor she must come." Polonius' "*Beautified* Ophelia," also suggests the ill repute in which feminine face decoration was held.

On the stage, since earliest times, make-up has been used for disguise and emphasis. The Greek masks may be regarded as a type of make-up. They took the form of grotesque representations of violent emotions: anger, revenge, hate, mirth. Our classic symbols of comedy and tragedy still remind us of this method of high-lighting the features.

Modern grease paints, first made in Germany, were at first looked upon with suspicion, as injurious to the skin. Perhaps they were, but now that they are made of guaranteed pure substances, they are not harmful to the skin.

The fine art of make-up consists of concealing itself as such. When it is emphasized to the point of recognition, it is poorly done. Its object is the illusion of health and beauty in straight roles, and natural lines of disguise in character.

Too little make-up is always preferable to too much.

A tin box is the best container for materials, as it keeps them from drying out prematurely.

New kinds of material are constantly being developed, but the purpose and the art of application remain the same. The most recent conveniences on the market are *tube* grease paints, and *dermatograph* pencils.

Grease Paints come in large sticks (Stein's) or in tubes (Factor's and Miner's). The colors range from number 1, which is the lightest juvenile, growing progressively deeper to about number 19, which is negro, to a number in the neighborhood of thirty. The remaining numbers label miscellaneous odd colors. The preceding statement applies particularly to Stein's brand. As each maker has his own system of numbering, the paints should be recognized by color rather than by number.

Lining Colors are put up in smaller sticks (Stein's), in small china jars (Factor's), or in dermatograph pencils, still made in only a few colors.

Powders are put up in tin cans, large and small, and are available in sixteen or more colors.

The following may be regarded as a fairly complete equipment for an ordinary make-up operation:

A Study in make-up.

1. Any large sheet to throw over the actor's clothing.
2. Cold cream.
3. Tissue, or cloths for wiping off cold cream.
4. Grease paints: five or six for women, four for men.
5. Liners: four shades for women, six for men.
6. Powders, to correspond to colors in grease paints.
7. Powder puffs, for dabbing on powder.
8. Face brush, for removing surplus powder and blending.
9. Hare's foot for applying dry rouge.
10. Mascara—various colors—for changing color of hair.
11. Crepe hair, for making beards—all natural colors.
12. Spirit gum for sticking on beards.
13. Dry rouge for hasty finishing touches.
14. Scissors for cutting crepe hair and trimming beards.
15. Nose putty for building up nose and face bulges.
16. Paper stomps, or toothpicks for making and blending lines.
17. Black enamel for blocking out, white enamel for whitening teeth.
18. Pins, adhesive tape, court plaster, for emergencies.
19. Derma pencils for convenience in lining.
20. Clown white for special effects.

With these articles, the artist is ready to proceed.

He seats his subject facing a strong light, and covers his clothing with a sheet.

He covers the face with cold cream, works it into all the pores, then wipes the surplus off with a soft cloth, or tissue, taking care to leave the skin slightly moist.

He selects the proper shade of grease paint to give the desired complexion, rubs off generous portions of the stick in several streaks across the face and neck, not forgetting the ears, then with finger tips stroking outward blends the streaks until the paint is evenly distributed.

Next he selects the quality of rouge in harmony with the ground color, rubs into each cheek a patch the size of a silver dollar, then delicately spreads this patch in all directions until the edges lose themselves in the ground color.

He remembers that:

A broad face may be made to look narrower if the rouge is placed close to the nose; a narrow face broader if the rouge is placed out toward the ears.

Youth takes rouge high on the cheek bone; old age low down along the lower jaw.

The best rouge area is where the roses naturally grow in youth and health.

He selects a lipstick to match and applies it, taking care to follow the natural ruby of the lips, unless he desires to change the shape of the mouth in some way. If lips are too full, he rouges only the inner portion; if too thin, he rouges a little outside the natural line. To make a wide mouth smaller, he carries the rouge to any desired distance short of the natural corners of the mouth; to make it wider he rouges to the corners and even beyond. He may turn the corners up or down to emphasize expression. He avoids the *cupid bow* mouth, unless a baby-doll effect is his object.

He brightens the face by placing a dot of red at the inner corner of the eye, and another dot at the nostril. He enlivens the expression by adding a suspicion of rouge just below the eyebrows.

Next he selects his liners: black for a decided brunette, light brown, or lake for light brunettes and dark blondes, light blue for very light features.

With an ordinary toothpick he scrapes a portion of the stick into his palm and, using his palm for a palette, he draws the pick through the color; then with the toothpick flatwise across the skin he draws his lines. He does not use the point of the pick, because it is liable to prick the skin, and because he gets a better line the other way.

If he has provided himself with dermatograph pencils, he saves himself the trouble of the toothpick process.

First, he lines the eyes, drawing a line just below the lower lid, and another just above the lashes of the upper lid. To enlarge the eye, he starts a little space from the inner corner and carries it any distance beyond the outer corner, according to the illusion of size he wishes to achieve. He brings the lower and upper lines together at the outer corner or any distance beyond. The size of the triangle of skin formed by the meeting of these lines will represent the effect of enlargement achieved. Where the small eye effect is desired, he lines more heavily toward the inner corner, leaving the outer corner natural.

The eyebrows are colored with the liner corresponding in color to the hair. Because extremely light brows do not show up on the stage, he makes them up darker than natural.

The shape of the brows determines the expres-

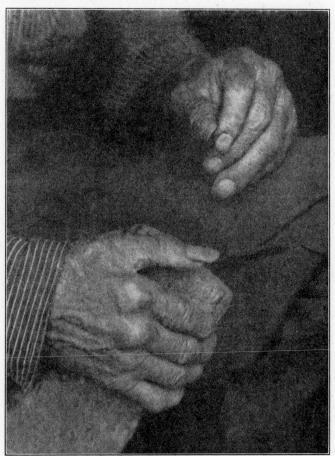

Old Hands.

sion of the face. He may block out the natural brows with tape and re-draw them to suit the character and expression desired.

In straight make-up, he is now ready for the powder. He selects a shade corresponding to the base, dabs it on generously, then blends it by brushing off the surplus gently with a baby brush or hare's foot.

Straight make-up is simple; it can be successfully applied by a student after a few rehearsals. The test for the artist comes in character make-up.

In this, the first few steps are the same as in straight make-up, except that the ground colors may need to be deeper, and the liner more carefully selected for individual effect.

If the face needs hair, he may use some made to order on gauze, or shape it out of crepe hair. He combs out a portion from the braid, clips it off with scissors, works it into any shape required, and sticks it on with spirit gum. If it must stand the test of very close inspection, he may unravel his braid, soak it in water to take out the crinkle, let it dry, and then apply it carefully hair by hair to the gummed surface. For more expeditious, and yet quite satisfactory work, he applies it untreated.

He may achieve a fairly good imitation of a moustache by rolling a bit of hair between his palms, further shaping the result with his fingers into two equal parts, cutting them apart, and pasting them on the upper lip on opposite sides of the groove. Or he may wish to imitate the kind that conceals the groove, in which case he does not clip the mass in two, but applies it in a unit.

A beard is made by teasing a portion of the hair into any shape desired, smearing the area to be covered with spirit gum, then firmly holding the hair to this area for a few moments to make sure that it sticks. Then he trims it carefully with the shears.

He knows that he can do much with hair to express character and nationality. He also knows that much practice is needed before anyone can hope to approach the illusion of reality.

Extreme old age is a matter of lines, high-lights, and shadows. If gray hair is needed, he fits it on. Then he proceeds to his lining.

He makes wrinkles with gray, brown, or lake, not black, unless he wishes very deep wrinkles and has time to blend them properly. He blends lines with gray or white. A thin line of dark color, high-lighted above, below, or both with white, gives the effect of a deep, fleshy wrinkle.

Unless he wishes to change the face, he follows the natural lines of the features. He draws more or less regular lines in the brow, short lines down along the nose from the inner corner of the eye, curving lines from the nostrils to the corners of the mouth, fine lines around the eyelids and lips to suggest shriveled appearance, crows' feet at the outer corners of the eyes, and any other lines that may make the character more individually real. He does not forget to line the throat and neck to bring out cords and hollows.

In old age the bony structure is likely to stand out and the fleshy portions to sag. Any color lighter than the base is a high-light; any color darker than the base would be a low-light. With the former he brings a feature into prominence; with the latter he subordinates it. He high-lights the cheek bones, jaw bones, and eye sockets, with carefully applied gray or white; he low-lights the sunken flesh with brown, dark gray, or purple.

Corpulent old age needs different treatment.

To understand character make-up, the student must study subjects from life, as well as carefully prepared charts and portraits.

Miscellaneous suggestions:

It is hard to make wrinkles look natural with black.

For shading above the eyes, if you must have it, use blue.

Make scars with crimson at center, brown around edges.

For youth, do not shade below eyelids, except to indicate illness.

Line hazel eyes with light green.

Line blue eyes with blue or lilac.

Horizontal lines broaden the face, vertical lines narrow it.

For Egyptian effect draw a line slightly beyond the point of meeting of the lid lines.

For oriental eyes slant the lines up to meet above the natural corner.

Unshaven effects may be secured with purple liner, with crepe hair finely cut, or with fine cut tobacco for tramps.

Beading the lashes is an unnecessarily harmful practice.

Stage darkeys are not black, but brown. Their lips are better left the natural color, as rouge looks artificial. Minstrels are conventionally black.

Old age is likely to have overhanging brows. These may be either artificial eyebrows made on gauze, or crepe hair pasted on over the natural brows.

The nose may be made to appear more slender by drawing a thin line down the ridge. A wide white line would tend to flatten it somewhat.

Any feature may be made more prominent by high-lighting, and exaggerations may be achieved with putty properly applied.

Straight make-up is as simple in application as street make-up, and both should be applied carefully. Properly blended coloring enhances the beauty of the wearer, but rouge put on in a patch suggests poor art, and still poorer taste.

The artificial lighting of the stage makes make-up a necessity. Some present day actors have undertaken to demonstrate the reverse, but have not completed the demonstration to the entire satisfaction of themselves, or of their audiences. A little make-up is advisable in cases of normal characterization, and abnormal characterization calls for much make-up applied with artistic ability.

Some amateurs do not like the smell of grease paint; others take great delight in it. Some young men cannot endure the odor and sting of spirit gum on their faces; others rather enjoy the sensation. With all, it is an acquired taste.

On the whole, make-up is great fun to put on, and greater fun to wear. It can be put on badly, which spoils the fun for everybody; or it can be done so well that the beholder enjoys the effect without being conscious of the process.

Make-up cannot be done well on the first or the second attempt. It takes patient practice after careful study.

In using Max Factor's or Miner's newest prod-

ucts, creaming the face may be omitted, except as
it may be needed to remove street make-up. The
Factor Studios publish, for distribution to patrons,
a series of very helpfully illustrated pamphlets on
make-up, progressing from the simplest to the most
intricate. They contain some portraits of conventional types, which might well serve as models for
students to copy in their own faces.

Wigs.—The wig, partly a detail of costume, and
partly of character, is hard to put on so that it appears natural. The wig line on the forehead will
obtrude, and the wearer's own hair will unexpectedly
crop out in spots, unless the wig fits perfectly and
is properly shaded into the skin of the forehead
with tissue and make-up.

There is more than one way to put a wig on, but
there is only one best way. It is best put on from
front to back. The forehead line is set firmly in
place, and the rest of the wig is drawn carefully
back and down at the sides until it covers every
part of the scalp.

When in place, the line of a partly bald wig may
be disguised with tape, and covered with a layer
of grease paint and powder. If it is not bald, this
line will be amply covered by the hair in most
cases.

The bald wig, then, would need to be put on
before the make-up, while other kinds may be ad-
justed at any time it is convenient.

In many cases, amateur actors may save much
trouble and expense by wearing their own hair,
and coloring it to order. Talcum powder, corn starch,
orris root, or any of the masques or mascaras on
the market will turn the trick.

ASSIGNMENTS

1. Make yourself, or a classmate, up for a straight part.

2. Find a good character portrait, and, using it as a model, try to copy it on your face.

3. Make up a face representing extreme old age—man or woman.

4. Find pictures of, and copy, four or five types of eyes expressive of temperament or nationality.

5. Make up your hand to represent hard-working old age.

6. Illustrate how shading and line may change the contour and the expression of the face.

7. Give your classmate a double chin.

8. Put a sword cut, or other scar onto your cheek.

9. Make up a jovial "Fezziwig" face.

10. Try a sour "Scrooge" expression.

CHAPTER XVI

COSTUMING

According to tradition, Eve devised the first costume in the Garden of Eden, preparatory to her debut into whatever society there may have been outside the gates of Paradise. Her son, Abel, being only a delver in the soil, probably wore some loose home-spun garments made out of the things he raised. His brother, Cain, a mighty hunter, naturally decked himself in skins of the animals he slaughtered.

The history of costuming is the history of man in his evolution from cave-dwelling days to this day of highly complex civilization, and in his settlements on lowland, mountain, inland, seacoast, islands of the sea, and from the Equator to the Poles.

So faithful is dress to the conditions of men that the clever costume designer needs only to know the period of civilization, the geographic locale, the occupation and social status of his subject in order to devise a dress that will be as near the truth as the stage can hope to come.

Viewed in this light, the study of costuming becomes something much more stimulating than mere contemplation of obsolete styles and decayed materials. The art assumes a significance aside from its stage purpose, and a man, as well as a woman, can adopt it as a career without feeling that he is reverting to the pre-Brunhild days.

186

Philip Merivale.

Many of our best costume designers are men. Strangely enough, these men can probably neither cut a pattern nor sew a seam. This simply means that the designing of a costume, and the execution of the design, are two separate departments in the process, just as outlining the specifications of a set of scenery and carrying them out may be the work of two differently gifted individuals.

In a general course in the stage arts, the theory of costuming would be interesting and valuable to all students. Practical application of the theory may be determined on the basis of aptitude and taste. The student of art might draw the designs, the student in clothing and textiles might work out the designs, and all might be asked to pass critical judgment on the result.

Sources.—If there ever were such a land as the lost Atlantis, we can never hope to learn how the people lived and dressed, because all records perished with the submergence of the land. If the story is more than fable, it is possible that pictures and inscriptions made on some water-defying material may some day be raised from the bottom of the sea. Such would be the only possible source, outside of fertile imaginations, of any knowledge of Atlantis costuming.

Writers of books on costuming have gone into the dusty dregs of history for their pictures and terminology. Ancient Egypt, Assyria, Babylon, Persia —all "did their days in stone," as Tennyson puts it. Any test on Ancient History is made vivid with illustrations taken from such inscriptions.

The student in costuming can do one of two things. If he is in haste, he may shy at extensive research, and take what some investigator has put

into a book for his convenience. Or he may choose
to go into the sources himself. The one would be a
student, the other a scholar. The first might learn
enough about costuming to serve his purpose as an
amateur director of plays; the other might uncover
new material that would throw light on more than
costuming.

Highly cultivated tastes are very fickle. Our
modern styles change without due notice, and in
response to most unaccountable whims. But styles
of the less progressive peoples stay approximately
as they always were. African and Asiatic nations
are fairly static in their apparel. The European
peasant, shut off from the influences of neighboring
nations, wears the same colorful dress his ancestor
invented thousands of years ago. The European
nobleman, more cosmopolitan in his relationships,
responds in his dressing to foreign influence. Thus,
the sheep herder of William The Conqueror's time
in England, described by Sir Walter Scott in *Ivan-
hoe*, would pass his costume down to his descendant
to the third, fourth, or fortieth generation; while
his more worldly master would reform his style several times in one generation.

Thus, the student of the stage, if he does not
care to specialize in costuming, must at least understand the philosophy of costuming, in order to be
impressed with the importance of dress in the interpretation of a play.

There are some old plays that absolutely demand
costuming in tune with their period, and other
equally old plays that do not. Anna Cora Mowatt's
Fashion would lose much of its punch without the
dress that belongs to 1845, but T. W. Robertson's
Caste, written only twenty years later, would suffer

very little distortion in modern dress. Shakespeare does not need to be dressed in any *one* way. One designer may devise one set of costumes for *Midsummer Night's Dream* that perfectly conveys the spirit of the play and carries the illusion; another may design costumes a considerable distance from the conventional, and still achieve an effect equally good, or even better. This is true of most of Shakespeare's plays, since the author himself bothered very little about being true to any period or any locale. The main idea in plays of this kind is to dress the actors in "the spirit of the times," and forget authenticity and convention.

Goldsmith's *She Stoops To Conquer,* and Sheridan's *The Rivals* and *School For Scandal* demand authentic costuming, as do most Colonial and Civil War plays. Here the period is definitely established, and the styles are generally understood and recognized. Every student knows the sort of gown Mrs. Malaprop would have worn, and can guess at her personal adornments. But very few people would be troubled by the costumes Romeo and Juliet wore, so long as they suggested the spirit of romance and medieval Italy. This statement is based upon the many delightful variations in Shakespearean costuming on our present day stage.

The important point to remember here is this: every play may be the better for being dressed in the style of the period in which it was written, but some period plays may be good in modern costume. The professional producer, who has money to invest in preparation for a long and remunerative run, would deserve to fail, if he were satisfied with anything short of detailed accuracy. But the amateur who prepares the play for one performance, and who has no "angel" to pay the bills, may be excused if he undertakes a good play without money for costuming. It is a question whether Ibsen's *A Doll's House*, or *Hedda Gabler*, loses anything at all by being dressed in modern style. On the other hand, *Peer Gynt* would stay as dead on the stage as he is in the book, if it were not for picturesque costumes and scenery.

"The apparel oft proclaims the man." What a man wears is a part of what he is, and like make-up, a garment may be of great aid in characterization. Costuming is an art in itself and it cannot be adequately taken up in a general discussion. All that can be expected of a book like this is that it give the student some idea of the problems of costuming. The first is to decide what the costumes should be. This is comparatively easy. A period play usually calls for costumes of the same period. Illustrations of these are readily found in old magazines, histories, portraits and books on the period.

The second problem is to get what we want. Funds for the purchase of the material may be lacking, or skilled labor for converting the material into wearing apparel may be hard to find. Fortunately, there are many supply houses willing to co-operate. Costumes may be rented. The difficulty is to get a good fit, and to secure the authentic article. Dealers are so anxious to do business that they send what they happen to have, which may be close to, or far from, what is wanted.

Another difficulty is that rented costumes are offered for one rehearsal and the final performance. This is hardly sufficient to enable an amateur actor to accustom his mood and behavior to the style of an unusual garment.

Genuine period costumes can often be borrowed from members of the community who happen to treasure them as heirlooms.

The best way is to make your costumes. This can be done if there is a capable seamstress to take charge, and several women who are willing to help. In a school group the instructor and students of the Domestic Science Department should be able and willing to undertake the work for the sake of training and experience.

Costumes are a visual description of time, place, and *character*. They must not only be accurate chronologically and geographically, but must also express the wearer's adopted personality physically and psychologically. They must be worn in the manner of the time, place and person. A young woman cannot very well wear a robe of Queen Elizabeth, and at the same time walk, stand or sit like this year's co-ed.

The actor's costume expresses him, *as he is to be* for the time being. He wears it, not so much to conceal his own body, as to *reveal* the body of his character. He must wear it to invest the part he plays with the *quality* of the personality he represents. The colonial costume, for instance, belongs to the minuet age, when all movements were graceful, sweeping, stately.

Illustrations of period costumes need not be copied literally, but may be skillfully adapted. Select only those elements of style that harmonize with the spirit of the play. If it is a farce, we may exaggerate some of the period features to get the farcical degree of grotesqueness. By artful emphasizing a flounce here, and subordinating a ruffle there, the costume not only remains faithful to the period represented, but also suggests the social standing of the characters, and the spirit of the play.

But the art of costuming does not concern itself with period plays alone. It covers the dressing of all plays. Important as the style of the garment may be, the color is even more vital. Colors speak louder than words in defining personality to the audience. The warm colors—reds, oranges, yellows —suggest health, life, and animal spirits. In some combinations, they may even hint at passion and vice. The cool colors—blues, greens, violets—suggest serenity, sweetness of character, and modesty of demeanor. White, like the lily, may suggest purity; black speaks of sorrow, gloom, mystery. Every color has a tongue that speaks to the spirit "ditties of no tone."

A well dressed cast shows a harmonious variety of color. White, black, pink, red, gray—any color combinations that do not clash too much and make effective contrasts. Two characters that are together, as much as Mrs. Allonby and Lady Stutfield in *A Woman Of No Importance*, should be gowned in colors of pleasing contrast. Moreover, Mrs. Allonby, a confirmed flirt, would be dressed in the warmest of warm colors. Hester, in the same play, naïvely unsophisticated, would wear white or the cooler colors, while Mrs. Arbuthnot, a victim of a tragic past, would best express her melancholy through black.

As has been hinted, the material for stage clothing need not be silks and satins, any more than the diamonds need be real stones. Any inexpensive stuff that can be dyed to create the illusion of richness will be highly satisfactory. Any good costume book will supply the details of the dyeing process, and any good drug clerk and dry goods merchant will be able to advise as to the kind of dye and the kind of material to use.

Materials are classified as to *weave* and *weight*.

Weave may be coarse or fine. Coarse: tarlatan, mosquito netting, fish net, toweling, straw matting, burlap, coarse muslin or marquisette, etc. Fine: chiffon, mull, gauze, cheesecloth, crepe de chine, voile, lawn, challis, etc.

Weight is classified as light and heavy. Light: silk crepe, crepe de chine, China silk, chiffon, mull, tulle, tarlatan, nets, laces, gauzes, cheesecloth, challis, muslin, etc. Heavy: velvet, plush, denim, some silk crepe, some satins, corduroy, flannel, unbleached muslin, turkish toweling, felt, jersey, cotton.

Some of these materials have luster; others are dull. Oil cloth in any color shines on the stage like polished armor plate.

There are at least three kinds of dye stuff a student should know: cotton or salt dyes; silk or acid dyes; and the basic dyes. The first is chemically right for linens and other vegetable stuffs, the second is right for silks and other animal products such as wool, and the third, the analine variety, gives luster to the goods. Drug stores now supply a dye called "Rit" which seems to be adequate for most amateur jobs. The directions for use are specific and need not be repeated here.

As previously hinted, amateur play budgets do not permit the use of silks and satins for the whole cast. Neither will it do to dress the principals in expensive fabrics, and let the others wear dyed goods. All characters, important or otherwise, must be clothed similarly in order to appear consistent.

Wigs constitute an important element in costuming as well as in make-up. They may be studied under either heading, or both. When we make up a character type, the wig used becomes a matter of individual character peculiarity. When dealing with a period play of the Colonial or Addison-Steele era, the wig becomes a part of the costume. As it is almost impossible for an amateur to make a convincing wig, and as it is not too expensive or difficult to rent one, establishing connections with a good wig maker is the best course to take here.

ASSIGNMENTS

1. Buy or borrow a doll with articulated joints, and take measurements in the following detail:

Neck; shoulder; width of chest; width of back; bust; waist; length of front from neck to waist; length of back from neck to waist; armscye; under arm to waist; hips; from waist to hip; length of skirt, front, side and back; outside arm from shoulder to elbow, and elbow to waist; inside arm; arm above elbow; wrist.

Read a period play, select a feminine role, and study the costume requirements.

Find bits of goods already colored, or get plain goods and dye according to need.

Cut the goods according to the measurements you have taken of your doll.

In actual costuming, patterns may be purchased and adapted to design by lengthening, shortening, etc. Can you manage in this way, or can you do your cutting according to your figures?

2. Review the effect of light on color, and apply to your costumed doll.

3. If you wish to make costuming your special course requirement, study carefully any or all of the following as you may be able to find them in

Stage Costuming: Agnes Brooks Young.

Costumes and Scenery for Amateurs: C. Darcy Mackay.

Costume: Mary Evans.
Historic Costume: Lester.
Costuming a Play: Elizabeth Grimball.
Historic Costumes for the Stage: Lucy Barton.

CHAPTER XVII

PRACTICAL DEVICES AND STAGE EFFECTS

In every amateur group there should be one member trained to serve as Jack of all trades, and master of those odd little tasks that no one else can do. A fireplace, a stairway, a trellis, or a rock may be needed, and someone must be found with ability and ingenuity enough to supply the demand. A simple formula, and an apt illustration, may suffice to start the clever young man on the right track.

The Fireplace.—We often see beautifully designed and perfectly executed fireplaces in professional productions. The amateur cannot achieve these and does not often need them. A well equipped college theatre usually already has all the accessories needed in an ordinary production. The student who anticipates directing plays, in out of the way places, must know how an article is most easily and inexpensively made.

The fireplace is a simple matter of frames put together. These may be covered with canvas and treated as in the case of flats; or they can be covered with one of the light composition boards now on the market. Determine how high and how wide the fireplace is to be in relation to the interior. Using the same strips of 1' by 2" white pine, make two frames, say, four feet high, six feet wide. Provide for the opening for the grate. The illustration will suggest the form of the framework.

The method of fastening these together may be

197

left to the individual. Clout nails may do the work, but screws will be more permanent. The mouldings and other ornamental devices may also be left to individual taste, and designed to serve the nature of the interior represented.

The Stairway.—Of course, any carpenter can construct a stairway according to specifications, but the amateur carpenter may find a great deal of satisfaction in doing it himself. The ordinary stair run consists of a supporting frame, the treads, and the risers. The tread is the board underfoot, the riser the upright board at right angles to it. Equipping the stairs with newel posts, rail, and balustrades is a more delicate job, and will call for some skill in manual craft.

Cut-Outs.—A cut-out is best made of material like beaver board cut to represent the object in mind, and attached to a framework that will support it solidly in place. Here the trick is mainly that of making the outline of the object realistic, and of painting it to create the desired illusion. A row of snow-capped peaks in the far distance against the color lighted cyclorama, for instance, calls for a cut-out of decidedly rugged outline to represent the horizon line of actual mountains seen far away. A large boulder close at hand would be another thing. Here the edges would have longer lines and curves and angles.

In all efforts to represent objects in nature, care must be taken to get the riot of natural color in rather bold, profuse streaks and masses. Reds, browns, yellows, greens, and blues are sometimes found in a single rock or tree trunk.

Rocks, trees and other objects seen in close perspective are better represented in three dimensions.

They are made by framework covered with canvas, and painted to create the illusion.

A tree may be made in any one of three ways: (1) Cut out of beaver board, painted, and attached to a tall frame that opens and closes like the jack used in supporting flats; (2) Made by winding chicken wire around a tapering frame, and covering this with canvas to be painted; (3) Made carefully and expensively in some such way as the carpenter makes a pillar. This last method would be particularly suitable for a clean, straight, tall tree.

A forest may be represented in many other ways. A stage production of O'Neill's *The Emperor Jones* employed masses of cloth shaped into the semblance of trees. Unfortunately, the lighting in some of the theatres where it played inadequately disguised the trick, and the illusion failed.

Every student of production should have a variety of tricks for creating special effects. He may be satisfied with those that have been used by others, or prefer to experiment and devise original and more convincing methods of reproducing sounds to accompany and motivate action.

The following are some of the conventional methods of securing special effects.

The Avalanche.—Sometimes, as in *Brand*, much depends upon the realism of the represented landslide. The light effects may be obtained by a disc, so constructed and so operated as to leave the stage intermittently dark and illuminated. Sound effects are subdued rumblings, an occasional crash subdued to suggest desired distance, and a rushing sound as of a mighty wind. These may be obtained by rolling bowling balls across the floor, subdued rumble on a bass drum head, and possibly an accompaniment on a wind machine. The crash may be done on the drum, or thundersheet.

Bells.—A door bell and a telephone bell are made in a conveniently portable box, or fastened to a piece of white pine 1″ x 6″ one foot in length. A bell and a buzzer are fitted into this and connected with a battery strapped to the wood. Any good electrician can make an easily portable bell and buzzer, or two bells of different ring.

Church bells, clocks, and chimes are produced by striking lengths of clean pipe with wood or steel. The pipe is suspended by a cord or wire to give off free vibrations. The quality of the sound will depend upon the thickness and the length of the pipe, and the nature of the percussion instrument. If the orchestra is equipped with chimes and a triangle, these sounds may be delegated to the musician.

Cow bells, engine bells, sleighbells, et cetera, can easily be the genuine article, as these can be found in any community with a little searching. They can be imitated with a carefully selected sounding iron. Devices yielding exact effects are on the market, and may be purchased at small or great cost, depending upon the article. For rare use, a home made device is quite satisfactory.

Crashes.—A broken window effect is produced by dashing a bag of broken glass to the floor.

Twigs breaking underfoot may be suggested by slats arranged in a rack so as to break under a lever pressed down over them.

Various other noises may be imitated convincingly in a variety of ways which the ingenious stage manager may discover for himself.

Fire.—Fireplace devices are on the market, but home made effects may be secured in several ways.

Hollowed out logs with openings in the bark and red or amber bulbs inside will make a respectable glow. Crumpled up black paper to represent coal shot through with red or amber light will suggest live embers.

Flames may be represented by red crepe paper stripped into ribbons, lighted with red or amber, and kept streaming with an electric fan.

Distant glow of a conflagration is effected through spotlights under the proper color medium—some shade of red, orange or yellow. The ebb and flow of the fire may be regulated by the dimmer.

Hoof Beats.—The traditional way of suggesting galloping or trotting horses is with halves of a dry cocoanut shell clashed against each other rim to rim, or against the floor or other resounding surface. Shod hoofs on cobble stones are particularly well suggested by this device. The manner and the rate at which these are worked will suggest the speed of the running horse.

Lightning.—An off stage flash may be simulated by winking a spotlight. Zig zag and other lightning patterns may be thrown on the background through openings cut into some opaque substance like cardboard. This is placed in front of a strong spot, which is switched on and off for each flash.

The Moon.—A black cylinder, a 1,000 watt lamp, and amber gelatine will yield a good suggestion of the moon. It is rather difficult to make the device move convincingly to represent the rising or the setting moon. It is perhaps more convincing to represent moonlight on the stage without the actual moon in sight. Moonlight blue gelatine will give the exact effect.

Motion.—Moving fire, wind, clouds, snow, etc. are

produced by special instruments that may be purchased or rented from supply houses. Because they are called for rarely, buying them would not be good economy, as many of them are very expensive. Renting them for occasional use is better business.

The *sciopticon* is very useful in throwing moving objects on the sky dome sheet. Clouds, sky colors, birds in flight, in short, anything that can be painted on a lens may be projected with this instrument. Actual moving picture films in small portable machines may be employed to secure some motion effects, but this is verging on hybrid art.

Rain.—Raindrops on clothing may be suggested by drops of glycerine.

The sounds of rain may be suggested:

By shot rolled over a drum head.

Shot or dry peas shaken in a fibre box.

Shot whirled in an empty cigar box will suggest a certain kind of rain effect.

These suggestions may suggest many others that will give the exact effect wanted.

The Rainbow.—This may be achieved by a properly placed prism, or by a special device procurable from a supply house.

The Sea.—The sound of waves may be suggested by peas or shot tipped back and forth in a canvas covered box eight feet long and one foot wide. The fury of the waves will be regulated by the rapidity and vigor of the tipping.

Shots.—These are best made with guns loaded with blanks. When more subdued effects are desired, or when guns are not easily to be had, a light plank pressed down to the floor with the foot, raised with the fingers and suddenly released will give the effect. The violence of the explosion will be regulated by the strength of the foot pressure. Two books slapped together might do, if they could be depended upon to meet always exactly flush face to face. On a small stage, where the audience is very close to the actors, a pistol shot is rather too intense to be comfortable. To be sure, if the gun is to be used on the stage in plain sight, no substitute is possible.

Smoke.—Smoke in the grate or stove may be produced with burning joss sticks or firecracker punk. Clouds of smoke may be suggested through color lighting, or some actual smudge that will be within the law of the fire ordinance. A chemist would know many harmless ways of producing vapor.

Snow.—Wet snow on clothing may be suggested by wet salt. Falling snow may be white paper, or confetti dropped from above. Driven snow seen through doors or windows may be mere light effects, or confetti driven by an electric fan and accompanied by a wind machine.

Stars.—Star designs are cut out in cardboard, placed before a spotlight and thrown on the sky sheet.

Sunset.—An olivette equipped to hold the gelatine frame is well suited to cast sunset glow, because it throws its rays parabolically. The particular colors of the sunset are secured through the appropriate colors in gelatine.

Thunder.—The rumbling kind is made with a thunder sheet: a piece of sheet iron, or heavy tin in any size convenient to handle. The larger the sheet, the deeper the thunder. Distant thunder may be suggested by rolling a cannon ball, or bowling ball across the floor. A good drummer can suggest a variety of roll and crash on his bass drum. A violent crash may be made by striking the thunder sheet a violent blow with a padded drumstick, and then shaking the sheet to suggest the after-roll.

Wind.—The conventional wind machine consists of a cylinder covered with canvas revolving in a wooden frame and turned by a crank. A cross piece of timber is fastened to the frame so as to press against the canvas. As the cylinder revolves the friction of the canvas against the wood makes the wind sound quite realistic. The violence of the wind is easily regulated by the rate of turning. In the absence of the wind machine the principle of friction between canvas and wood may be worked out in a variety of ways.

The suggestions given above are by no means exhaustive. Effects not mentioned may be called for, and effects described may be secured in other ways. Those given should serve to point out ways and means of discovering the desired effects. An ingenious property man is quite equal to inventing special devices according to the requirements of the play. The electrician, by a little experimentation, can reproduce startling effects in original ways. The effect is to be as close to nature as possible, and there may be no one best way to produce it. The very best way may be waiting for some amateur to discover.

CHAPTER XVIII

GLOSSARY OF STAGE TERMS

It is a great satisfaction to the worker in any art to know its special terminology. The following definitions will not only acquaint the student with the technical language of the theatre, but also refresh his mind concerning the material discussed in preceding chapters.

Abstract Setting. A setting in which natural forms are so modified as to lose their natural significance.

Act Curtain. The curtain which cuts off the stage picture between acts.

Act Drop. The same as act curtain, or an extra lighter drape behind it.

Acting Area. The part of the stage reserved for the actors within the scene limits.

Apron. The portion of the stage extending in front of the proscenium frame.

Architectural Stage. A stage with a permanent architectural background.

Arm Cyclorama. A drop attached to battens hinged at right angles to the rear wall and used for masking the wings of the stage, as the backdrop masks the rear openings.

Asbestos. The fireproof curtain in front of the act curtain, required by law since the disastrous fire in the Iroquois Theatre in Chicago, December 29, 1903.

Atmosphere. The suggestive emotional effect of scenery, action, or vocal quality.

Back Drop. A curtain lowered as the rear limit of the acting area, or as masking for the rear wall openings.

Back Flap. A hinge with removable pin.

Backing. Any piece of standing or hanging scenery used

to limit the space seen through wall openings. It may represent the sky, a hallway, or another interior.

Back Stage. The space behind the scenery, out of the visual angle at the audience.

Back Wall. The rear wall of the interior set.

Balcony. The second floor of the auditorium, sometimes called *first balcony.*

Batten. A length of pipe or of wood suspended from the gridiron, and carrying a drop, or other hanging unit. Also one of the pieces forming the narrow side of the flat.

Batten-Clamp. A piece of hardware used for fastening hanging scenery to the batten.

Black-Out. A term used for switching off lights.

Blend. To harmonize more or less closely any elements in scene design, as adjacent colors, or color with light.

Book-Ceiling. A ceiling constructed on the principle of the flat, with two parts which together cover the set so hinged together as to close like a book.

Border. A width of masking material which hides the upper part of the stage space. It masks the border lights, and, in the absence of a ceiling, it may be used in place of it.

Box-Set. A setting composed of three walls and a ceiling.

Bring-Up. To raise the intensity of lighting.

Business. A term used to designate any action on the stage during the performance of the play. It is visible interpretation.

Cable. The insulated cord connecting lighting apparatus with the current.

Ceiling-Cloth. Cloth covering the ceiling frame.

Chalk Snapline. A chalked cord used for snapping straight lines between two points.

Clear Stage. A command meaning that the stage be cleared of all persons except the actors who are to figure in the scene.

Clout-Nail. A nail with easily bent point used in clinching pieces of wood together, particularly for fastening corner blocks and keystones across joints of the flat frame.

Cold Colors. Colors so named because of their supposedly unexciting emotional effect, as Blue, Green, Violet.

Color Frame. A steel or tin frame for holding color medium in front of the light apparatus to produce color effects in light.

Color Sketch. A design complete in line and color.

Color Wheel. A circle with colors marked off on it in the order of derivation sequence. Also a circular color frame arranged on the same sequence.

Constructivism. A style of stage craft in which substantial acting structures, angles, wheels, trellis and trestle work take the place of decorative design.

Convertible Unit. A unit of scenery constructed to lend itself to a variety of uses.

Corner Block. A triangular bit of three-ply used to clout joints of flats together.

Counter-Weight System. A system of weights used to balance units of scenery suspended from the gridiron.

Cover Off. Mask off, or furnish with backing.

Cradle. Container for ballast in the counterweight system.

Cut-In. A painted line used to create the illusion of a raised surface in scenery, as moulding, baseboard, etc.

Cut-Out. A ground row.

Cyclorama. A variously constructed scene unit made to represent the sky. Now often used to designate any drape set.

Decor. A foreign word used to indicate the entire setting, including the furniture and decorations.

Designer. The artist of the theatre who furnishes plans for setting, costumes, and color in keeping with the spirit of the play.

Dim. Reduce the intensity of light.

Dimmer. A device for reducing the current. The rheostat.

Director. The individual who has charge of the entire process of production.

Dock. Storage space for scenery.

Dome. The rounded upper portion of the cyclorama.

Door Flat. The unit of scenery provided with an opening for the door frame.

Down Stage. Towards the footlights.

Draftsman. The artist who prepares the working designs for the stage carpenter.

Drapes. Hanging units of scenery.

Draw Curtain. A curtain that opens and closes laterally.

Drop. Any curtain lowered from above, whether used as scenic background, or cut-off for scene change.

Dutchman. A device used in the construction of three-folds to permit complete folding.

Earth Colors. Products of earth substances, as ochre, sienna, umber.

Expressionism. The style of production in which natural scenic background is subordinated to symbols expressive of the meaning or connotation of the play.

Finish Off. To complete the painting of the set by working in the final details.

Fireproofing. Treating scenery with a fireproof substance.

Flat. A unit of standing scenery.

Flies. The space above the stage. The fly gallery.

Floodlight. A boxed reflector giving intense unfocussed light.

Floor Cloth. Canvas covering for the floor of the acting area.

Floor Pocket. An opening in the floor for light plug.

Fly Gallery. The platform from which ropes controlling various hanging units are manipulated.

Flyline. A continuous rope beginning at the pin rail, running through pulleys, and fastened to the battens that carry hanging scenery.

Flyman. The man who manipulates scenery from the gallery.

Foot Iron. An iron with an eye at the lower end of the stage brace through which the stagescrew is fastened to the floor.

Footlights. The row of lights arranged in a trough in front of the curtain in the apron floor.

Forestage. The apron.

Formalism. Setting the stage with forms that represent an universal reality rather than a definite locality.

Front. The auditorium and box office.

Funnel. A flue for carrying smoke in case of fire.

Gallery. The second balcony.

Gauze. Theatrical scrim. Netting used for mist and haze effects.

Glaze. A thin coat of paint applied in the toning process.

Grass Mat. A mat of artificial grass used in exterior sets.

Grid, Gridiron. The frame work in the space above the stage.

Grip. The scene shifter.

Ground Color. The first solid coat of paint applied to scenery, or in make-up.

Ground Row. A piece of scenery resting on the floor without being attached to another unit, used to represent irregularities in topography.

Hand Props. Small properties carried by actors in their business.

Hanging Scenery. Units of scenery suspended from above and lowered into place.

High Light. To paint the suggestion of light on objects. In make-up, touching up any part of the face with color lighter than the base.

Hokum. A cheap theatrical trick for easy effectiveness.

House. The auditorium.

House Lights. Auditorium lights.

Hue. Color in its full intensity.

In One, Two, Three. Scene set in the first, second, or third part of the stage. Borrowed from obsolete wing system.

Inscenierung. A German term without English equivalent, meaning the entire environment of the actor. *Decor.*

Intensity. The degree of brightness in a hue.

Jack. A device for bracing standing units, a triangular leg hinged to the back of the flat, which when open, keeps the flat from falling backwards.

Jog. A narrow flat used to break the regularity of wall line.

Keeper-Hook. An S-shaped hook slipped over toggle-bars of adjoining flats and holding a batten for keeping the flats edge to edge.

Keystone. A piece of three-ply used to clout the joints of toggle-bars and cross piece to stiles and battens of the flat.

Lash. To fasten flats together edge to edge with a cord attached to the upper corner and thrown around cleats placed zig zag fashion along the stiles.

Lash Line. The cord used in lashing flats together.

Lash Line Cleat. The metal spur screwed into the stile around which the lash line is thrown.

Lay-In. To apply the first coat of paint to scenery.

Left Stage. The part of the acting area at the actor's left as he faces front.

Leg-Drop. A hanging unit of scenery composed of border and wings in one piece.

Light Pocket. A space within the lighted area where there is no light. A light void.

Lock Off. To lock down the line of the counterweight system.

Long Line. The line attached to the farther end of hanging scenery.

Louvres. Circular strips of metal in certain types of lighting appartus which send the rays out parallel.

Macbeth Trap. A trap in the stage floor which can be opened and shut quickly.

Mahl Stick. A stick held in one hand used to guide the other hand in painting lines.

Make-Up. Material used to accentuate features, or to disguise personality. It is a name applied to the material, to the process, and to the result indiscriminately.

Mask. Backing for scenery.

Masque. Cosmetic materials.

Medium. Color gelatine substance used to color the light.

Mise-en-Scene. A French phrase meaning the "getting up of a dramatic piece."

Mood. The emotional effect of the setting, or performance.

Motif. A symbol of expression. The theme, or dominant tone of a work.

Multiple-Unit-Set. A set of flats that may be re-combined to yield any number of settings.

Naturalism. A style of playwriting and production attempting to represent actuality in body and spirit.

Off Stage. Outside the acting area of the stage.

Olivet, Olivette. A portable open box reflector.

Paint Bridge. A platform, usually in the flies, built along a wall for the painter to stand on when painting scenery.

Paint Frame. A frame for hanging scenery on the wall for the purpose of painting.

Parallel. The supporting unit in a platform stage.

Pattern. The orderly composition of forms.

Perspective. Representation of the third dimension of an object.

Perspective Sketch. A sketch representing the scene in all its dimensions.

Picture Frame Hook. A special device attached to the top of a picture—a hook which slips into a frame socket on the wall.

Pigment. Color in its basic form.

Pin Hinge. A hinge with a removable pin, like a door hinge.

Pin Rail. A timber in the flies to which lines are fastened.

Plastic Stage. A stage built up to several area levels, all of which may serve both as decorative effect and acting areas.

Practical. Any unit of scenery which is employed in stage business.

Practical Unit. A piece used by actors in their business.

Primaries. Basic colors. Hues: Red, Yellow, Blue. Light: Red, Green, Violet.

Properties. Furniture and articles that help to make the stage a practical environment for the actors in their work of interpreting the play.

Property Table. Table in the wings where hand properties are placed ready for the actor's use.

Proscenium. The architectural partition between the stage and the auditorium.

Proscenium Arch. The opening in the proscenium.

Rail. The external wooden member of a flat. A batten.

Rake. The angle of opening of a set toward the audience.

Raking Piece. Another name for the ground row.

Ramp. A sloping platform flush with the stage floor.

Regisseur. Master director.

Returns. Any units of scenery which cover the opening between the front edges of the walls of the set and the sides of the proscenium wall.

Reveal. The thickness of the wall as shown by the depth of door and window frame.

Revolving Stage. A circular stage floor arranged on bearings so that any part of it may be brought into the proscenium opening and instantly utilized as acting area.

Rhythm. Movement marked by regular recurrence of emphasis. In stage design and stage picture, a pleasing variety of regularly recurring motif; in line, color, grouping and action. (See illustrations.)

Right Stage. Actor's right as he faces front.

Rises. The vertical distances between the treads of stairs.

Roll-Ceiling. A ceiling spread over separable rails and rolled up when not in use.

Running a Flat. Sliding a flat in vertical position in shifting scenery.

Scale. The mathematical relation between a drawing and its life size model.

Scenery. The actor's environment.

Scumbling. Touching the canvas gently with the tip of an almost dry brush. A method of painting.

Set-Up. Assembling the setting.

Shade. A variation of hue resulting from an admixture of black.

Sheave. The grooved ring of a pulley.

Shift. Scene change.

Short Line. The line attached to the end of the drop nearest the pin rail.

Sill Iron. The metal strip in the bottom of the door in a door flat.

Size. To apply a mixture of glue, whiting and water as the preparatory coat in painting scenery.

Sky Dome. The sky sheet, or plaster surface representing the sky.

Spatter. A method of stippling which consists of dashing the paint on with brush tapped across the wrist.

Spotlight. A strong light with reflector and focusing lens.

Stage Brace. An adjustable batten with hook at one end and foot iron at the other, used in making flats stand rigid.

Stereopticon. A device for projecting pictures on the sky sheet.

Stile. The upright strip of wood in the flat frame.

Strike. A command to scene shifters to take down the set.

Strip Light. A detachable trough of light units.

Tab Backing. A drop lowered behind the tableau curtain.

Teaser. A border used to cut down the height of the proscenium opening.

Template Bench. A carpenter's bench used for making flats uniform.

Thickness Piece. A piece of timber in a frame that shows reveal.

Three-Fold. Three flats hinged together with two way hinges.

Tie Off. To make fast a fly line.

Toggle Bar. Any piece of lumber within the flat frame; a cross piece which the shifter grips in running a flat.

Toning. Bringing colors into harmony by typing them with other colors.

Tormentors. Properly, the open space between the proscenium arch and the returns. The returns themselves.

Trap. An opening in the stage floor.

Tread. The horizontal surface of a stair step.

Trimming. Adjusting borders to make them hang parallel to the floor.

Tripping. Doubling up a backdrop to make it come only half-way down.

Two-Fold. Two flats hinged together.

Up Stage. Acting area near the rear wall.

Value. The degree of tint or shade in colors.

Vehicle. The liquid used to dissolve pigment powder.

Vibrate. To create the effect of motion in light or setting.

Wagon Stage. A stage on wheels that can be brought within the proscenium opening already for the actor.

Walk It Up. To raise a flat to vertical position.

Warm Colors. Reds, Oranges, Yellows.

Window Flat. A flat containing an opening for the window frame.

Wing Nut. A bolt furnished with a nut with spurs for easy manipulation with the fingers.

Wings. A system of flats set along the sides of the stage parallel to the rear wall. The sides of the stage outside the acting area.

Wood Wing. A wing flat representing a woodland scene.

APPENDIX A

PRODUCIBLE PLAYS

Since of the making of plays there is no end, any list, however complete today, will miss all the good plays published tomorrow. The present list is made up from among the plays that happen to be in the compiler's office, most of them furnished gratis by publishers for his state Loan Library. Represented are Samuel French; Walter Baker; Row, Peterson; Longmans, Green; Northwestern; Bugbee; Dramatic Publishing Company; Dennison; Ingram; Fitzgerald; and many who publish plays only incidentally. Since any of these furnish the plays of all, the name is not listed after each play.

Plays are graded loosely: I, II, III. Grade I represents plays of the most difficulty in production, of highest literary worth, or of a prohibitive degree of sophistication. Grade II includes most of the professional stage successes calling for a royalty of twenty-five dollars or more, most of them worthy of the efforts of both college and high school. Grade III designates plays low in royalty and, in too many instances, low in dramatic quality. By no means all are recommended to groups capable of doing better work.

The following symbols will further define the plays: C, comedy; D, drama, including tragedy; F, farce; Md, melodrama; Fy, fantasy; My, mystery; Mu, musical: #, large, indefinite number in the cast.

The number of *sets* is given in place of *acts*.

Play	Author	Type	Sets	Men	Women	Grade
Abraham Lincoln	Drinkwater	D	6	#	#	I
Absent-minded Judy	Braun	C	1	5	5	III
Accent on Youth	Raphaelson	C	1	6	3	I
Accusing Finger	Doran	My	1	5	7	III
Ace High	McMullen	C	1	4	5	III
Across the Street	Purdy	F	3	7	3	III
Adam and Eva	Middleton-Bolton	C	2	6	4	II
Adam's Apple	Dalton	F	1	6	3	III
Addie Sails Away	Maibum	C	1	8	6	III

214

Play	Author	Type	Sets	Men	Women	Grade
Adding Machine	Rice	Fy	7	14	11	I
Admirable Crichton	Barrie	C	2	9	6	I
Adventures of Grandpa	Hare	F	1	5	4	III
Adventures of Lady Ursula	Hope	C	4	12	3	III
After Wimpole Street	Braun	C	1	4	6	III
After You I'm Next	Worcester	C	1	5	8	III
Agatha's Aunt	Toler	C	1	5	5	II
Alarm Clock	Hopwood	C	1	4	4	II
Alice in Wonderland	LeGallienne	Fy	#	#	#	II
Alice Sit-by-the-Fire	Barrie	C	2	3	6	I
Alicia Perks Up	Pierce	C	2	4	3	III
Alien Corn	Howard	D	1	11	3	I
All in the Family	Stone	F	1	8	6	III
Allison Makes Hay	Helburn	C	1	7	7	II
Allison's House	Glaspell	D	2	5	6	I
All-of-a-Sudden Peggy	Denny	C	2	6	5	II
Altogether Reformed	Kaufman	C	1	7	6	III
Always Count Ten	Spence	C	1	7	11	III
Amazons	Pinero	C	2	9	5	II
American Citizen	Ryley	C	3	9	5	II
American Very Early	Lackaye	C	1	9	10	III
Among the Breakers	Baker	C	1	6	4	III
Among the Stars	Wayne	C	1	9	4	III
Among the Winners	Doran	C	1	3	7	III
And Let Who Will be Clever	Nash	C	1	5	7	III
Androcles and the Lion	Shaw	F	2	#	#	I
Angel Cake	O'Ryan	C	1	3	8	III
Animal Kingdom	Barry	D	2	5	4	I
Anna Christie	O'Neill	D	4	10	2	I
Ann's Little Affair	Osborne	C	1	4	4	III
Ann What's Her Name	Hare	C	1	7	10	III
Another Language	Franken	C	2	6	5	II
Another Spring	Sprague-Wayne	D	1	5	7	II
Anything Might Happen	George	F	1	6	6	III
Apple Blossom Time	Hafer	C	1	5	7	III
Applesauce	Conners	C	2	2	3	II
Arabian Nights	Grundy	F	1	4	5	III
Are You a Mason	Dietrichstein	C	1	7	7	II
Aren't We All	Lonsdale	C	2	8	4	II
Argyle Case	O'Higgins	My	3	14	5	II
Ariadne	Milne	C	1	3	4	II
Arms and the Man	Shaw	C	2	6	3	I
Arnold Goes Into Business	McMullen	C	1	8	6	III
Arrival of Kitty	Swartout	C	1	4	5	III
Art of Being Bored	Pailleron	C	1	11	9	II
As Husbands Go	Crothers	C	3	7	5	I
As the Clock Strikes	Armstrong	My	1	5	6	II
As the Leaves	Giacosa	C	1	5	6	II
At Mrs. Beam's	Munro	C	2	3	7	II
At 9:45	Davis	My	3	10	5	II
At Yale	Davis	C	4	16	4	II
Aunt Cindy Cleans Up	Braun	F	1	4	7	III
Aunt Emma Sees It Through	Farndon	F	1	4	3	III
Aunt Sally and the Crime Wave	Short	C	1	4	6	III

Play	Author	Type	Sets	Men	Women	Grade
Aunt Samanthy Rules Roost	George	C	1	5	6	III
Bab	Carpenter	C	3	7	4	II
Baby Cyclone	Cohan	F	3	9	5	II
Bachelor's Honeymoon	Stapleton	C	1	4	8	II
Bachelor's Romance	Morton	C	3	11	7	II
Backing Into Eden	Mansfield	C	2	8	4	III
Bad Boy Comes Back	Short	C	1	5	5	III
Bad Man	Browne	Md	1	10	2	II
Barbara Frietsche	Fitch	D	4	13	5	I
Barber of Seville	Beaumarchais	C	2	9	1	II
Barretts of Wimpole Street	Besier	D	2	13	5	I
Bat	Rienhart-Hopwood	My	2	7	3	II
Battle Hymn	Blankfort-Gold	D	4	#	#	I
Be an Optimist	Applebud	C	2	6	7	III
Beau Brummel	Fitch	D	4	12	7	I
Beauty Shoppe	Van Der Veer	C	1	5	7	III
Be Calm Camilla	Kummer	C	3	6	3	II
Before Morning	Ryley	My	1	7	4	III
Beggar on Horseback	Kaufman-Connelly	Fy	5	16	5	I
Behind the Throne	Brighouse	C	3	6	3	II
Behold We Live	Van Druten	C	2	4	4	I
Believe Me Xantippe	Ballard	C	3	7	3	II
Belinda	Milne	C	2	3	3	I
Berkeley Square	Balderston	Fy	2	7	8	I
Best People	Gray-Hopwood	C	2	9	5	II
Beverly's Balance	Kester	C	3	5	4	II
Beyond the Horizon	O'Neill	D	3	6	4	I
Be Yourself	Braun	C	1	5	6	III
Big Brother	Allyn	C	1	4	4	III
Big Hearted Herbert	Kerr-Richardson	C	1	7	6	II
Big Idea	Hamilton-Thomas	C	3	7	4	II
Big Lake	Riggs	D	4	7	3	I
Big Pond	Middleton-Thomas	C	2	4	5	II
Big Time	Adams	C	3	11	9	III
Billeted	Jesse-Harwood	C	1	4	5	III
Bill of Divorcement	Dane	D	1	5	4	I
Billy	Cameron	C	1	8	5	II
Biography	Behrman	C	1	5	3	I
Bird In Hand	Drinkwater	C	2	6	2	I
Bird's Christmas Carol	Wiggin	Fy	2	7	7	II
Bishop Misbehaves	Jordan	F	2	7	3	II
Black and Blue	Orwig	C	3	7	4	III
Black Coffee	Christie	My	1	10	3	II
Black Eye	Bridie	C	6	11	9	I
Black Flamingo	Janney	My	1	9	4	I
Blossoming of Mary Ann	Short	C	3	4	8	III
Blow Your Own Horn	Davis	C	1	8	5	III
Blue Bag	McMullen	F	1	6	5	III
Blue Ghost	McEwen-Riewerts	My	1	6	1	III
Blue Ribbon Pie	Monsell	C	1	0	9	III
Blundering Herd	Holmes	C	1	6	5	III
Bobbie Take a Look	Bridgham	C	1	6	8	III
Bonds of Interest	Benevente	C	4	11	6	I
Boomerang	Smith-Mapes	C	2	6	5	II
Boss	Sheldon	D	4	13	4	I
Boston Blues	Perrine	C	1	8	6	II
Both Your Houses	Anderson	D	3	13	3	I

Play	Author	Type	Sets	Men	Women	Grade
Bought and Paid For.....	Broadhurst.......	D	3	4	3	I
Box and Cox............	Morton..........	F	1	2	1	III
Boy Meets Girl........	Spewacks.........	F	#	#	#	I
Boy Through the Window..............	Clements.........	C	1	3	3	III
Brass Buttons...........	Luce.............	C	1	0	7	III
Brat..................	Fulton...........	C	1	4	7	III
Breezy Money..........	Todd............	F	1	10	0	III
Brewster's Millions......	Smith............	C	3	19	6	II
Bridal Chorus...........	Winter...........	C	1	8	6	II
Bride..................	Oliver-Middleton..	C	1	7	2	II
Bride the Sun Shines On...	Cotton...........	C	1	8	5	II
Bringing Up Father......	Brandon.........	F	1	5	7	III
Broadway Jones........	Cohan...........	F	3	11	4	II
Broken Dishes..........	Flavin...........	C	1	6	4	II
Broomsticks Amen.......	Greenfelder.......	C	1	6	4	II
Brown of Harvard.......	Young...........	C	2	29	4	II
Brown's In Town........	Swan............	C	1	5	4	II
Bunco Man.............	Refling..........	C	2	7	4	III
Bunty Pulls the String....	Moffat...........	C	2	5	5	II
Burglary At Browne's....	Shute............	C	1	7	4	III
Busy Body.............	Davis............	F	1	8	8	III
But Katydid...........	Wayne...........	C	1	7	5	III
Butter and Egg Man.....	Kaufman.........	C	3	8	5	I
Call Me Mike..........	Reach-Taggart....	F	1	6	6	III
Canaries Sometimes Sing.	Lonsdale.........	C	1	2	2	I
Candida................	Shaw............	C	1	4	2	I
Candlelight............	Wodehouse.......	C	1	5	3	III
Cappy Ricks...........	Rose............	C	2	6	3	II
Captain Applejack......	Hackett..........	Fy	2	6	5	I
Captain Jinks.........	Fitch............	C	2	13	13	I
Captain Kidd..........	Young...........	C	1	12	3	II
Captain Letterblaire.....	Merington........	C	3	8	5	I
Case of Rebellious Susan..	Jones............	C	#	10	4	I
Case of the Squealing Cat..................	Reach...........	My	1	8	6	III
Cassilis Engagement.....	Hankin..........	D	1	4	8	II
Caste.................	Robertson........	Md	2	5	3	II
Cat and the Canary......	Willard...........	My	2	6	4	II
Caught In the Rain......	Collier...........	C	1	12	11	III
Cave Girl.............	Middleton-Bolton..	C	2	7	3	II
Celebrity..............	Jerome...........	C	2	5	4	II
Champion.............	Louden-Thomas...	C	1	13	4	II
Character Intrudes......	Costello..........	C	1	7	3	III
Charley's Aunt..........	Thomas..........	F	2	7	4	II
Charm................	Kirkpatrick.......	C	2	7	5	II
Charm School..........	Miller-Milton.....	C	2	6	10	II
Cheating Cheaters.......	Marcin...........	C	3	9	4	II
Cherokee Nights.......	Riggs............	D	7	#	#	I
Cherry Orchard........	Capek...........	D	2	8	5	I
Chicken Feed..........	Bolton...........	C	1	7	4	II
Children of the Moon....	Flavin...........	D	1	5	3	I
Children's Hour........	Hellman..........	D	2	2	12	I
Chinese Lantern........	Hausman.........	Fy	1	12	2	II
Choice................	Sutro............	D	3	6	5	I
Christopher Junior.......	Ryley............	C	3	8	4	II
Cinderella Man.........	Carpenter........	C	2	8	3	II
Circle................	Maugham........	C	1	4	3	I
Clarence..............	Tarkington.......	C	2	5	5	II

Play	Author	Type	Sets	Men	Women	Grade
Clean-Up	Conners	C	1	4	5	II
Climbers	Fitch	D	2	12	9	I
Clover Time	Worcester	C	1	5	6	III
Cock Robin	Barry-Rice	My	2	8	5	I
Cocktails or Tea	Jones	C	2	4	6	II
College Cinderella	Kidder	C	1	4	8	III
College Widow	Ade	F	4	15	10	I
Come Easy	Metcalfe	C	1	5	5	II
Come Out of the Kitchen	Thomas	C	3	6	5	II
Come Seven	Cohen	C	1	6	7	III
Come What May	Flournoy	C	2	9	3	II
Comic Supplement	Braun	C	1	3	6	III
Comin' Thru the Rye	George	C	1	5	8	III
Commencement Days	Frame-Mayo	C	2	6	9	II
Company's Coming	Wilson	C	1	9	6	III
Connie Goes Home	Carpenter	C	1	4	5	II
Constant Wife	Maugham	C	2	4	5	I
Contrary Mary	Ellis	C	2	7	5	III
Copperhead	Thomas	D	3	9	5	I
Coquette	Abbot-Bridges	D	1	7	4	I
Corner of the Campus	Gale	C	3	6	10	III
Corney Breaks Record	Osgood	C	1	2	10	III
Cosy Corners	Phelps-Short	C	2	4	7	III
Counsellor at Law	Rice	D	2	19	9	I
County Chairman	Ade	F	4	16	5	I
Courting	Matthews	C	1	4	4	III
Cousin Kate	Davies	C	1	3	4	II
Crab Apple	Packard	C	1	5	2	II
Cradle Song	Sierra	D	2	4	10	I
Craig's Wife	Kelly	D	1	5	6	I
Creaking Chair	Wilkes	My	1	8	4	II
Cricket on the Hearth	Dickens-Brown	Fy	2	5	10	II
Crime at Blossoms	Shairp	My	1	12	10	II
Crisis	Churchill	D	3	14	8	I
Cuckoo's Nest	Cottman-Shaw	F	1	6	5	III
Cupid at Vassar	Davis	C	3	4	9	III
Cupid Scores a Touchdown	Osgood	C	1	3	7	III
Cyrano de Bergerac	Rostand	D	5	37	11	I
Daddies	Hobble	C	2	6	8	III
Daddy	Smith	C	2	4	4	II
Daddy Longlegs	Webster	C	4	6	7	II
Daisy Mayme	Kelly	D	1	3	5	I
Dangerous Corner	Priestly	D	1	3	4	I
Dating Lady Luck	Hill	C	1	8	3	II
Daughters of Atreus	Turney	D	3	14	15	I
David Copperfield	Dickens-Linda	D	2	6	7	II
Death Takes a Holiday	Casella	Fy	1	7	5	I
Deirde of the Sorrows	Synge	D	3	8	3	I
Devil in the Cheese	Cushing	Fy	#	7	2	I
Devil's Disciple	Shaw	Md	3	9	3	I
Devil's Host	Glick	My	1	8	3	II
Diamonds	Allyn	C	1	3	6	III
Dictator	Davis	Md	3	14	3	I
Digging up the Dirt	Morton	C	1	6	5	III
Dinner at Eight	Kaufman-Ferber	C	6	14	11	I
Disraeli	Parker	D	4	14	6	I
Distaff Side	Van Druten	D	2	5	8	I
Dodsworth	Lewis-Howard	D	#	10	8	I

Play	Author	Type	Sets	Men	Women	Grade
Doll's House	Ibsen	D	1	5	4	I
Dollars and Chickens	Ballard	C	1	6	3	II
Dolly Reforming Herself	Jones	C	1	6	3	I
Don	Besier	D	2	4	5	I
Don Quixote	Cervantes-Kester	C	3	4	7	I
Don't Count Your Chickens	Braun	C	1	0	13	III
Don't Darken My Door	Martens	C	1	3	5	III
Dorothy's Neighbors	Doran	C	3	4	7	II
Dorothy Vernon	Kester	D	4	9	6	I
Double Door	McFadden	D	1	8	4	I
Double Trouble	Reach	F	1	6	7	III
Dover Road	Milne	C	1	6	3	I
Dragon's Teeth	Quin	D	1	5	4 Ex.	I
Dulcy	Kaufman-Connelly	C	1	8	3	II
Dumb Dolliver	Todd	F	1	6	4	III
Dummy	O'Higgins-Ford	C	3	9	2	II
Dutch Detective	Hare	F	1	5	5	III
Dybbuk	Ansky	D	#	#	#	I
Dying to Live	Braun	F	1	4	7	III
Dynamo	O'Neill	D	4	4	3	I
Eagle Screams	Braun	C	1	6	6	III
Earl of Pawtucket	Thomas	C	3	15	3	I
Earth	Fagan	D	4	11	3	I
East Lynne	Wood	D	2	7	7	I
East of Suez	Maugham	D	7	5	4	I
Easy Come Easy Go	Davis	C	3	11	5	II
Easy Money	Goetz	F	1	5	6	III
Easy Payments	Hobart	C	3	10	5	II
Eldest Son	Galsworthy	D	3	17	4	I
Eliza Comes to Stay	Esmond	C	1	5	4	II
Elizabeth the Queen	Anderson	D	3	17	4	I
Elopement of Ellen	Warren	C	2	4	3	III
Emperor Jones	O'Neill	D	6	3	1	I
Emperor's New Clothes	Chorpenning	C	1	#	#	III
Enchanted April	Campbell	C	2	5	5	III
Enchanted Cottage	Pinero	Fy	2	5	4	II
Enemy	Pollock	D	1	7	3	I
Enemy of the People	Ibsen	D	4	9	2	I
Engaged	Gilbert	F	2	6	4	III
Engaged By Wednesday	Owen	C	1	5	11	III
Enter Madame	Varesi-Gray	C	1	5	5	II
Errand for Polly	Duncan-Matthews	C	1	9	7	III
Erstwhile Susan	DeForest	C	1	8	9	II
Esmeralda	Burnet-Gillette	D	3	9	4	II
Eternal Magdalene	McLaughlin	D	1	9	4	I
Eternal Spring	Garland	D	1	4	3	II
Eternally Yours	Braun	C	1	4	5	III
Everybody Getting Married	Moore	C	2	7	7	III
Excuse Me	Hughes	C	2	16	5	II
Excuse My Dust	Reed	C	1	4	6	III
Expressing Willie	Crothers	C	2	6	5	II
Facing the Music	Darnley	F	1	5	4	III
Fall Guy	Abbot-Gleason	C	1	7	2	II
Family Upstairs	Delf	C	1	4	5	II
Famous Mrs. Fair	Forbes	C	2	3	10	II
Fanny and Servant Problem	Jerome	C	1	3	17	II

Play	Author	Type	Sets	Men	Women	Grade
Fanny's First Play	Shaw	C	3	5	3	I
Farmer's Wife	Phillpots	C	2	10	11	II
Fashion	Mowatt	Md	2	8	5	II
Fast Workers	Oliver	F	1	5	4	III
Father and the Boys	Ade	C	4	10	6	I
Father Walks Out	Furniss	C	2	5	4	II
Fickle Fortune	Shute	C	2	4	8	III
Field God	Green	D	1	5	7	I
Finnegan's Fortune	Townsend	C	1	5	3	III
First Lady	Dayton-Kaufman	C	2	13	12	I
First Man	O'Neill	D	2	6	7	I
First Mrs. Fraser	Ervine	C	1	4	4	I
First Year	Craven	C	2	5	4	II
Fixing It for Father	McMullen	C	1	5	3	III
Flour Girl	Phelps-Short	C	2	4	4	III
Flowers of the Forest	Van Druten	D	2	6	5	I
Fly Away Home	Bennet-White	C	1	7	6	III
Following Father	Franklin	C	1	8	4	II
Fool	Pollock	D	3	13	8	I
Fool's Gold	Conners	C	1	10	5	II
For Love of Mike	Maltby	F	1	6	3	III
Fortune Hunter	Smith	C	4	17	4	I
Fourflusher	Dunn	C	2	8	5	II
Fourth Wall	Milne	My	1	8	3	I
Foxy Mrs. Foster	Brandon	C	1	5	6	III
Fresh Fields	Novello	C	1	2	7	II
Friend Hannah	Kester	C	2	7	4	II
Friendly Enemies	Hoffman	C	1	4	3	II
Front Page	Hecht-MacArthur	Md	1	17	5	I
Full House	Jackson	F	1	7	7	II
Full of Youth	Braun	F	1	5	9	III
Gasoline Gipsies	Stewart	C	1	4	4	II
Gay	Loving	C	1	3	6	III
Gay Co-Eds	Doran	C	1	5	7	III
Gay Reunion	Vees	C	1	8	7	III
Gentle Rogue	Brownell	C	1	11	4	II
Ghost Train	Ridley	My	1	7	5	I
Gingham Girl	Kussel-VonTilzer	Mu				II
Gipsy Trail	Housum	C	2	5	4	II
Girl from Child's	Colby-Jackson	F	1	4	6	II
Girl In a Thousand	Whiting	D	1	0	4	III
Girl of the Golden West	Belasco	Md	4	21	5	I
Girl With Green Eyes	Fitch	C	3	10	17	I
Glee Plays the Game	Gerstenberg	C	1	0	14	III
Goblin Gold	Mackay	C	2	4	5	III
Going Crooked	Smith-Collier	C	1	8	3	III
Going Some	Armstrong	D	3	12	4	II
Golden Days	Toler-Short	C	3	3	7	II
Gold Mine	Matthews-Jessup	D	1	7	2	II
Golf Champ	Goetz	F	1	4	6	III
Good-Bye Again	Haight-Scott	C	1	8	4	I
Good Gracious Annabelle	Kummer	C	3	10	4	II
Good Hope	Heijermans	D	s	11	7	I
Good Listener	Reach	C	1	5	7	III
Good Morning	Gibbs	C	1	9	7	II
Good News	Schwab-DeSylva	Mu	7	10	5	I
Goose Hangs High	Beach	C	1	7	5	II
Grand Hotel	Baum	D	1	16	5	I
Grandma Gets a Job	Doran	C	1	3	7	III

Play	Author	Type	Sets	Men	Women	Grade
Graustark	McCutcheon-Hayward	Md	3	9	4	II
Gray Wraith	Sutherland-Kiser	My	1	7	2	III
Great Adventure	Bennett	C	3	15	3	I
Great Divide	Moody	D	3	11	3	I
Greater Commandment	Maxwell	C	1	5	3	III
Great God Brown	O'Neill	D	7	9	3	I
Green Bay Tree	Shairp	D	2	4	1	I
Green Ghost	Reach	My	1	6	6	III
Green Goddess	Archer	Md	3	7	2 Ex.	I
Green Grow the Lilacs	Riggs	D	6	10	4 Ex.	I
Green Light	Schimmel	My	1	12	4	III
Green Pastures	Connelly	Fy	#	#	#	I
Green Phantom	Spence	My	1	6	6	III
Green Stockings	Mason	C	1	7	7	II
Grouch	Torrey	C	1	5	9	III
Growing Pains	Rouverol	C	1	8	10	II
Grumpy	Hodges-Percival	Md	2	9	3	II
Guess Again	Hughes	F	1	8	6	II
Gun Shy	Little-Closser	C	1	7	3	II
Hail Nero	Stocks	C	3	12	5	I
Hairy Ape	O'Neill	D	7	6	5	I
Hamilton	Arliss	D	3	11	5	II
Happiness for Six	Hughes	C	1	3	3	III
Happy Go Lucky	Hughes	F	1	6	6	III
Happy Prodigal	Denny	C	2	6	6	II
Harlequinade	Barker	Fy	4	11	2	I
Harvest Moon	Thomas	D	4	6	4	I
Haunted House	Davis	My	1	8	3	II
Have Patience Doctor	Ball-Scribner	C	1	8	4	III
Hawk Island	Young	Md	1	8	5	II
Hay Fever	Coward	D	1	4	4	I
Hazel Kirke	Mackaye	Md	2	9	5	I
Healthy, Wealthy, Wise	George	F	1	6	9	III
Heart of the Shamrock	Rosener	C	1	4	4	III
Heart of Paddy Whack	Crothers	C	2	6	6	II
Heart Trouble	Chenery	C	1	5	5	III
He Comes Up Smiling	Ongley	C	1	10	4	II
Hedda Gabler	Ibsen	D	1	3	4	I
He Had a Past	Spence	C	1	0	7	III
He Landed from London	Lee	C	1	4	5	III
Held By the Enemy	Gillette	D	4	14	3	I
Hell Bent fer Heaven	Hughes	D	1	5	2	I
Hello Bill	Goodhue	F	1	6	5	III
Here Goes the Bride	Wayne	C	1	6	6	III
Her Friend the King	Thomas-Rhodes	C	1	6	5	II
Her Husband's Wife	Thomas	C	1	3	3	II
Her Incubator Husband	Spence	C	1	4	7	III
Her Master's Voice	Kummer	C	2	3	4	II
Her Moving Picture Hero	Spence	F	1	6	9	III
Her Own Way	Fitch	D	3	5	9	I
Her Temporary Husband	Paulton	C	2	4	2	II
Her Western Romeo	Toler	C	1	5	8	II
He Who Gets Slapped	Andreyev	D	1	20	13	I
Hickory Dickory	Nichols	C	2	10	4	III
High Tor	Anderson	Fy	1	5	3	I
Hindle Wakes	Houghton	D	2	4	5	I
His Excellency, Governor	Marshall	F	1	10	3	III

Play	Author	Type	Sets	Men	Women	Grade
His House In Order	Pinero	D	2	10	4	I
His Majesty Bunker Bean	Dodd	C	4	12	6	I
His Women	Sprague	C	1	0	9	III
Hobgoblin House	Tobias	My	1	6	5	III
Hobson's Choice	Brighouse	C	2	7	5	II
Holiday	Barry	C	2	7	5	II
Home	Cooke	D	2	5	2	III
Honeymoon	Bennett	C	1	6	2	III
Honor Bright	Nicholson	C	1	9	6	III
Hoodoo	Hare	C	2	6	13	III
Hotel Universe	Barry	Fy	1	5	4	I
Hottentot	Mapes	F	2	8	3	II
House Beautiful	Pollock	D	#	7	5	I
House Next Door	Manners	D	2	8	4	II
House of Connolly	Green	D	3	4	6 Ex.	I
House of Seven Gables	Spence	D	1	11	11 Ex.	II
How Dare You	Spence	C	1	7	6	III
How's Your Health	Tarkington	C	2	8	6	II
Huckleberry Finn	Twain-Lewis	C	1	4	6	II
Hullabaloo	Schafner	C	1	4	3	III
Hurlbut the Great	Reed	C	1	5	5	III
Hurry, Hurry, Hurry	Arnold	C	1	6	3	III
Icebound	Davis	D	1	5	6	II
Ideal Husband	Wilde	C	2	9	6	II
Idiot's Delight	Sherwood	C	1	17	8	I
If I Were King	McCarthy	D	3	20	9 Ex.	I
I'll Leave It to You	Coward	C	1	4	6	I
I'll Remember You	Reach	C	1	6	6	III
Imaginary Invalid	Moliere	C	1	8	4	II
Importance of Being Ernest	Wilde	F	3	4	5	II
In Abraham's Bosom	Green	D	7	9	3	I
In a Garden	Barry	D	1	4	2	I
Inner Circle	Harvey	My	1	8	4	III
Innocent Ann	Stanley-Matthews	C	2	5	5	II
Inside the Lines	Biggers	D	2	11	5	II
In the Next Room	Robson-Ford	My	2	8	3	II
In the Shadow of a Rock	Conkle	D	1	9	6	I
Intimate Strangers	Tarkington	C	2	4	4	II
Invitation to a Murder	King	My	1	8	5	II
In Walked Jimmy	Jaffa	C	2	10	2	II
Irresistible Marmaduke	Denny	C	2	5	5	II
Is Zat So	Gleason	C	3	9	5 Ex.	II
It Happened In June	Hafer	C	1	4	5	III
It Never Rains	Rouverol	C	1	5	7	II
It Pays to Advertise	Megrue	C	2	8	4	II
It's Great to Be Young	Doran	C	1	3	7	III
It's Human Nature	Blackmore-Smith	C	1	8	3	III
It's Papa Who Pays	Cunningham	F	1	6	6	III
It's Turrible to Be Popular	Stafford	F	1	5	7	III
It Won't Be Long Now	Gropper	C	1	9	5	III
Ivory Door	Milne	Fy	2	11	4	I
Jack Straw	Maughm	F	2	9	3	II
Jade God	Barry	My	1	6	4	II
Jade Necklace	Short	My	1	3	5	III
Jane Clegg	Ervine	D	3	3	2 Ex.	I
Janice Meredith	Rose-Ford	D	3	21	3	I

Play	Author	Type	Sets	Men	Women	Grade
Jerry	Cushing	C	2	5	3	II
Jewell Robbery	Bloch	C	1	9	3	III
Jinx	Braun	F	1	5	8	III
Joan of Arc	Stevens	D	10	32	3	I
Jobyna Steps Out	Baumer	C	1	4	5	III
John Ferguson	Ervine	D	1	7	2	I
John Glaydes Honor	Sutro	D	3	7	5	I
Johnny Grows Up	Sprague	C	1	5	5	III
Johnny Johnson	Green	D	10	#	#	I
Jonesy	Morrison-Touhy	C	1	8	5	II
Journey's End	Sheriff	D	1	10	0	I
Judsons Entertain	Ellis	C	1	5	6	II
Judy Drops In	Swan	C	1	6	3	II
June	Doran	C	1	4	8	III
June Moon	Lardner-Kaufman	C	3	7	5	I
June Time	Shute	C	1	3	4	III
Juno and the Paycock	O'Casey	D	1	14	5	I
Justice	Galsworthy	D	5	17	1	I
Just Like Judy	Denny	C	1	4	5	II
Just Out of College	Ade	F	3	15	11	I
Just Suppose	Thomas	C	1	6	2	II
Kangaroos	Mapes	C	1	6	8	II
Keeping Up With Jane	Doran	C	1	7	7	III
Keep Off the Grass	George	F	1	6	8	III
Kempy	Nugent	C	1	4	4	II
Key of the Door	Lowe	D	2	9	4	II
Kick-In	Mack	Md	2	7	5	II
Kind Lady	Chodorov	My	1	6	8	I
Kindling	Kenyon	D	1	6	4	I
King Rides By	Snook	C	1	6	6	III
Laburnum Grove	Priestly	D	1	6	3	I
Ladies In Waiting	Champion	Md	2	0	9	HI
Ladies of Creation	Unger	C	1	5	4	II
Ladies of the Jury	Ballard	C	2	12	10	II
Lady Epping's Law Suit	Davies	C	3	12	7	I
Lady Frederick	Maugham	C	2	8	5	I
Lady of Letters	Bullock	C	1	5	7	II
Lady Precious Stream	Hsiung	Fy	4	8	5	I
Lady Windermere's Fan	Wilde	D	2	7	6	I
Laff That Off	Mullaly	C	1	4	3	II
Lake	Massingham	D	2	4	5 Ex.	I
La Locandiera	Goldoni	C	3	4	4	II
Last of Mrs. Cheney	Lonsdale	D	3	8	6	I
Last of the Ruthvens	Barbee	My	1	5	6	III
Last Warning	Fallon	Md	2	10	4	II
Late Christopher Bean	Howard	C	1	5	4	I
Launcelot and Elaine	Royle	D	4	9	9	II
League of Relations	Osborne	C	1	6	5	III
League of Youth	Ibsen	D	3	11	7	I
Leave It to Polly	Bridgham	C	1	1	10	III
Leave It to Psmith	Wodehouse	C	4	10	8	II
Leavenworth Case	Ring	My	1	5	8	III
Left Bank	Rice	D	1	8	7	I
Lena Rivers	Albert	D	1	6	7	II
Let's Get Rich	Reed	C	2	11	5	III
Let Us Be Gay	Crothers	C	2	7	5	I
Libel	Wooll	Md	1	11	3	I
Life Begins At Sixteen	Manning	C	1	6	9	III
Lightnin'	Bacon	C	2	12	12	II

Play	Author	Type	Sets	Men	Women	Grade
Lilies of the Field	Turner	C	2	4	7	II
Liliom	Molnar	Fy	4	16	4	I
Lion and the Mouse	Klein	D	3	10	8	I
Listen to This	Doran	C	1	5	5	III
Listen World	Savage-LePeltret	C	1	5	5	III
Little Clown	Hopwood	C	2	8	7	III
Little Grey Lady	Pollock	C	3	6	5	II
Little Journey	Crothers	C	1	8	7	II
Little Men	Ravold	D	1	9	3	III
Little Miss Dreamer	Reach	C	1	7	7	III
Little Miss Fortune	George	C	1	4	7	III
Littlest Rebel	Peple	D	4	16	3	II
Little Teacher	Smith	C	2	11	10	III
Little Things	McMullen	C	1	5	5	III
Little Women	Alcott	D	3	4	7	II
Locked Room	Ashton	My	1	9	4	II
Lone Eagle	Roach	D	1	6	6	III
Look Who's Here	George	C	1	3	6	III
Loose Ankles	Janney	C	1	6	7	II
Loose Moments	Savage-Hobbs	C	1	4	8	II
Lottery Man	Young	C	3	4	5	II
Louder Please	Krasna	C	1	12	3	II
Love Expert	Kirkpatrick	C	1	5	5	III
Love Inc.	Else	C	1	7	4	III
Love on the Dole	Greenwood	C	3	9	7	II
Love Test	Judge	C	1	7	3	III
Lower Depths	Gorki	D	1	15	5	I
Loyalties	Galsworthy	D	3	17	3	I
Lucky Accident	Braun	F	1	4	7	III
Lucky Break	Sears	F	1	9	9	II
Lucky Dip	Vosper	C	1	8	4	II
Lucky Girl	Howard	F	1	6	8	III
Lucky Sam McCarver	Howard	D	4	15	5	I
Lunatics At Large	Reach	F	1	7	5	III
Lysistrata	Aristophanes	F	1	22	18	I
McMurray Chnn	Strachan	C	1	4	7	III
Madam Magnificent	Short	C	1	4	5	III
Mad Honeymoon	Conners	C	2	9	4	II
Mad Hopes	Brent	C	1	8	5	II
Madras House	Barker	C	2	#	#	I
Magda	Suderman	D	2	6	8	I
Magistrate	Pinero	F	2	12	4	II
Mail Order Brides	McMullen	C	1	7	6	III
Makropoulos Secret	Capek	D	3	6	6	I
Mamma's Affair	Butler	C	3	3	4	II
Mamma's Baby Boy	George	F	1	4	7	III
Maneuvers of Jane	Jones	C	3	9	11	I
Man of Honor	Landman	C	2	6	3	II
Man of the Hour	Broadhurst	D	4	13	2	I
Man on the Box	Furniss	C	2	11	4	II
Man from Home	Tarkington	C	2	11	4	II
Man from Nowhere	Allyn	C	1	5	5	III
Man from Texas	Dickerson	C	1	4	5	III
Man's World	Crothers	C	4	7	1	II
Mantle of Lincoln	Dalton	D	3	9	3	II
Mantuan	Moore	D	6	#	#	II
Man With Load of Mischief	Dukes	C	3	3	3	II
Man Without Country	Hale	D	3	22	2	I

Play	Author	Type	Sets	Men	Women	Grade
Marco Millions	O'Neill	D	#	29	3	I
Margie	Hilton	C	1	5	6	III
Marriage of Kitty	Lennox	C	2	4	3	II
Martha By the Day	Lippman	C	3	5	5	II
Mary Goes First	Jones	C	1	8	4	II
Mary Jane's Pa	Ellis	C	1	7	5	II
Mary Rose	Barrie	Fy	2	5	5	I
Mary's Ankle	Tully	F	2	6	4	II
Mary the Third	Crothers	D	2	5	5	I
Master Builder	Ibsen	D	2	4	4	I
Mater	McKaye	C	1	3	2	II
Maytime In Erin	Rose	C	2	6	3	III
Meal Ticket	Nicholson	C	1	6	6	II
Meet the Duchess	Reach	C	1	4	7	III
Meet the Wife	Starling	C	1	5	3	I
Me, Him, and I	George	C	1	5	7	III
Melting Pot	Zangwill	D	2	5	5	I
Menonite Maid	Howe	C	1	7	4	II
Merchant Gentleman	Moliere	C	3	9	7	II
Merely Mary Ann	Zangwill	C	3	8	6	II
Merry Death	Braun	F	1	5	7	III
Merry Madness	Gibney	C	2	8	5	II
Merton of the Movies	Kaufman-Connelly	F	5	7	4	I
Message from Mars	Ganthony	D	2	14	8	I
Mice and Men	Ryley	C	4	7	5	II
Michael and His Lost Angel	Jones	D	3	10	6	I
Michael and Mary	Milne	C	3	10	6	I
Mile a Minute	Davis	C	3	7	5	II
Milestones	Bennett	D	3	10	3	I
Milky Way	Clork	C	1	7	2	II
Mill of the Gods	Todd	D	2	4	4	III
Millionaire	Tompkins	C	1	4	5	II
Minnick	Crothers	C	1	6	9	II
Mishaps of Minerva	Porter	F	1	5	8	III
Misleading Lady	Goddard-Dickey	D	2	11	5	II
Miss Efficiency	Toler	C	2	8	4	II
Miss Hobbs	Jerome	C	3	5	5	II
Miss Lulu Bett	Gale	C	2	4	5	I
Miss Nell of N'Orleans	Eyre	C	1	3	5	II
Missing Witness	Reach	Md	1	14	8	III
Miss Somebody Else	Short	C	2	6	10	III
Miss Washington	Browne	C	2	5	4	II
Miss Yankee Doodle	George	F	1	6	9	III
Mistakes At the Blakes	LePelley	F	1	6	7	III
Mitzi Mixes In	Todd	F	1	4	5	III
Money In the Family	Fraser	C	1	4	5	III
Money to Burn	Nugents	C	1	4	5	II
Monsieur Beaucaire	Freeman	C	3	14	7 Ex.	I
Moon Over Mulberry Street	Courtney	C	1	6	6	II
Moonshine and Honeysuckle	Vollmer	C	1	8	5	II
Moonstone	Spence	My	1	9	8	III
Mother Carey's Chickens	Wiggins	C	1	7	7	II
Mother's Millions	Barnes	C	1	7	4	III
Mountain Mumps	Goetz	F	1	6	6	III
Mr. Antonio	Tarkington	C	2	8	7	II
Mr. Bob	Baker	C	1	3	4	III

Play	Author	Type	Sets	Men	Women	Grade
Mr. Faithful	Dunsany	C	2	11	2	I
Mr. Lazarus	O'Higgins-Ford	My	1	3	3	II
Mr. Pim Passes By	Milne	My	1	4	4	II
Mrs. Bumstead Leigh	Smith	C	1	6	6	II
Mrs. Dane's Defense	Jones	D	2	8	4	I
Mrs. Dot	Maugham	C	3	8	4	I
Mrs. Gorringe's Necklace	Davies	C	1	5	5	II
Mrs. Leffingwell's Boots	Thomas	C	2	9	5	II
Mrs. Temple's Telegram	Wyatt	C	1	4	5	II
Mrs. Wiggs of Cabbage Patch	Rice	C	3	15	11	I
Murdered Alive	Braun	My	1	5	7	III
Murder Has Been Arranged	Williams	My	1	4	5	II
Murder on the Second Floor	Vosper	My	2	6	4	II
Murray Hill	Howard	C	1	4	4	II
Music Master	Klein	D	3	14	6	I
My China Doll	George	Mu	2	10	10	II
My Friend from India	Souchet	F	2	7	5	II
My Lady's Dress	Knoblauch	Fy	#	#	#	I
My Lady's Shawl	Crandall	D	1	0	#	II
My Mother-In-Law	Braun	C	1	4	6	III
Mysterious Mrs. Updyke	Short	C	1	5	7	III
Mystery At Midnight	Allyn	My	1	5	5	III
Nancy Ann	Heyward	C	2	7	9	III
Nancy Pretends	Phelps	C	2	8	6	III
Napoleon Junior	Hershey	C	1	6	6	III
Nathan Hale	Fitch	Md	3	14	5	I
Ned McCob's Daughter	Howard	D	2	8	2	I
Nellie Was a Lady	Savage	C	1	5	5	III
Nervous Miss Niles	Short	C	1	4	4	III
Nervous Wreck	Davis	F	3	9	2	II
New Brooms	Craven	C	2	9	4	I
New Co-Ed	Doran	C	2	4	5	III
New Fires	Burdette	C	1	6	9	III
New Henrietta	Smith-Mapes	C	3	9	4	II
New Morality	Chapin	C	2	4	3	II
New Poor	Hamilton	F	1	6	6	III
Newspaper Bride	Short	C	1	3	4	III
New York Idea	Mitchell	C	3	9	6	II
Night Hostess	Dunning	C	1	12	5	I
Night of January 16	Rand-Reed	Md	1	11	10	II
Nine Till Six	Stuart	C	1	0	#	III
Niobe, All Smiles	Paulton	C	1	5	9	III
Noah	Obey	Fy	3	5	4 Ex.	I
Nobody's Home	Short	C	1	5	4	III
No Father to Guide Them	Else	C	1	4	5	III
None So Blind	Owen	C	1	4	6	III
No References Required	Barbee	C	1	5	7	III
Nose for News	Powell	C	1	9	5	III
Not Herbert	Young	My	3	7	5	II
Nothing But the Truth	Montgomery	F	2	5	6	II
Not So Fast	Westervelt	C	2	5	4	III
Not So Long Ago	Richman	C	3	5	7	I
Novel Princess	Burns	F	3	10	6 #	III
Number 17	Farjeon	My	4	7	2	I
Nut Farm	Brownell	C	1	6	4	II

Play	Author	Type	Sets	Men	Women	Grade
Officer 666	MacHugh	F	1	9	3	II
Of Thee I Sing	Kaufman-Ryskind	Mu	11	29	9 #	I
Oh, Clarissa	Reach-Taggart	F	1	6	5	III
Oh, Kay	Applebud	C	1	6	5	III
Old Fashioned Girl	Ravold	D	1	4	9	III
Old Lady 31	Crothers	C	2	4	10	II
Old Maid	Wharton-Akins	D	3	5	9	I
Old P. Q.	O'Higgins-Ford	C	1	8	3	II
Oliver Twist	Dickens-Ravold	D	1	10	7	II
Once In a Lifetime	Kaufman-Hart	F	5	24	14	I
Once There's a Princess	Tompkins	C	1	3	7	II
Once Upon a Time	Crothers	C	3	4	4	II
One Mad Night	Reach	My	1	7	7	III
One of the Family	Webb	C	2	4	6	II
On the Bridge At Midnight	Brandon	Md	1	5	8	III
One Sunday Afternoon	Hagan	C	3	12	7	I
Only 38	Thomas	C	2	6	6	II
On Stage	Kaye	C	1	6	2	II
On the Hiring Line	O'Higgins-Ford	C	1	5	4	II
On the Stairs	Hurlbut	C	2	7	3	II
Our Betters	Maugham	C	2	7	4	I
Our Boarding House	Braun	F	1	4	6	III
Our Mutual Friend	Dickens	C	2	4	4	III
Out O' Luck	Cushing	C	1	17	1	II
Out of the Night	Hutchinson-Williams	My	1	5	2	II
Outward Bound	Vane	My	1	6	3	I
Over the Hills	Browne	D	1	5	4	III
Over the Rainbow	Homer	C	1	4	5	III
Paddy the Next Best Thing	Page	C	3	6	9	I
Page Asa Bunker	Kavanaugh	C	1	6	4	III
Pair of Sixes	Peple	C	2	8	4	II
Pair of Silk Stockings	Harcourt	C	2	8	6	II
Pair of Spectacles	Grundy	C	1	8	3	III
Pals First	Dodd	C	2	8	3	II
Panther's Claw	Goetz	My	1	6	6	III
Paradise Lost	Odets	D	1	20	7	I
Paragraph for Lunch	Savage	C	1	6	6	III
Party's Over	Kussel	C	1	5	6	II
Passers-By	Chambers	C	1	4	4	II
Passing of Brompton Road	Thomas	C	1	4	5	II
Passing of Third Floor Back	Jerome	C	1	6	6	II
Pastures New	Johnston	D	2	7	6	III
Path of Glory	Peach	C	2	10	4	II
Patsy	Conners	C	1	3	3	II
Peaceful Valley	Kidder	C	3	7	4	II
Peer Gynt	Ibsen	D	#	#	#	I
Peggy Parks	St. Clair	C	1	6	5	III
Peg O' My Heart	Manners	C	1	5	4	II
Penelope	Maugham	C	3	6	4	I
Penrod	Tarkington	C	3	13	5	II
Perfect Alibi	Milne	My	1	7	3	I
Perfect Getaway	McMullen	C	1	8	6	III
Personal Appearance	Riley	C	1	4	6	I
Peter Pan	Barrie	Fy	#	11	4 #	I

Play	Author	Type	Sets	Men	Women	Grade
Peter Flies High	Fagan	C	1	8	6	II
Petrified Forest	Sherwood	D	2	17	3	I
Petticoat Fever	Reed	C	1	6	4	II
Petticoat Influence	Grant	C	2	5	3	II
Pigeon	Galsworthy	D	2	7	2	I
Phantom Bells	St. Clair	My	1	5	5	III
Phantom Claw	Goetz	My	1	6	6	III
Phantom Tiger	St. Clair	My	1	6	6	III
Philippa Gets There	Paulton	F	1	5	6	II
Pickles Becomes a Lady	Manning	C	1	5	9	III
Poor Little Rich Girl	Gates	D	6	9	10	I
Pillars of Society	Ibsen	D	3	10	9	I
Piper	Marks	D	5	13	6 #	I
Playboy of Western World	Synge	C	1	7	5	II
Play's the Thing	Molnar	C	1	8	1	I
Point Valaine	Coward	D	2	6	11	I
Polly of the Circus	Mayo	C	2	8	6 #	II
Polly With a Past	Middleton-Bolton	C	2	7	5	II
Polly Preferred	Bolton	C	#	8	3	II
Pomander Walk	Parker	C	1	10	8	I
Poor Nut	Nugents	C	1	11	5	II
Poor Simp	Covington-Mayo	C	1	10	8	II
Post Road	Steele-Mitchell	My	1	7	8	I
Poppa	Cohen-Spewack	C	2	10	5	II
Porter House Steak	Wayne	C	1	6	5	III
Pride and Prejudice	Jerome-Alcott	D	4	10	16	I
Pretty Sister of Jose	Burnett	D	2	10	5	I
Porgy	Heyward	D	#	#	#	I
Prince Chap	Peple	C	2	6	6	II
Prince There Was	Cohan	C	3	7	6	II
Princess and Mr. Parker	Seiler	C	2	#	# *	II
Private Secretary	Hawtry	C	2	9	4	II
Professor's Love Story	Barrie	C	2	7	5	I
Professor's Daughter	Bunner	C	2	5	4	III
Prunella	Housman	Fy	1	22	#	II
Pursuit of Happiness	Langner	C	1	8	3	I
Queen's Husband	Sherwood	C	1	11	4	II
Quality Street	Barrie	C	2	11	8	I
Quest of Happiness	Davis	Fy	1	#	#	III
Quincy Adams Sawyer	Adams	C	3	8	7	II
Quite a Remarkable Person	Brace	D	3	12		III
Rafferty Racket	Chenery	C	1	5	6	III
Rainbow Girl	Goetz	C	1	4	7	III
Rain from Heaven	Behrman	C	1	6	4	I
Rale McCoy	McKeown	My	1	4	3	III
Ralph Roister Doister	Udall	F	#	1	5	I
Rat Trap	Coward	D	3	3	4	I
Rear Car	Rose	C	1	8	3	II
Rebecca of Sunnybrook Farm	Wiggin-Thompson	C	5	4	9	II
Red-Handkerchief Man	Mann	D	1	#	2	III
Regatta	McKennan	C	1	6	6	III
Rejuvenating Aunt Mary	Warner	C	3	7	6	II
Remember the Day	Higley-Dunning	C	4	13	12	II
Return of Peter Grimm	Belasco	Fy	1	8	3	I

* One child.

Play	Author	Type	Sets	Men	Women	Grade
Reunion In Vienna	Sherwood	C	2	22	6	I
Right You Are	Pirandello	D	2	7	7	I
Rise of Silas Lapham	Howells-Sabine	D	3	12	8	I
Rival Ghosts	Osgood	C	1	5	4	III
Rival Masqueraders	Goetz	C	1	8	7	III
Rivals	Sheridan	C	#	8	5	I
Robina In Search of Husband	Jerome	C	1	8	4	II
Road to Yesterday	Dix-Sutherland	Fy	3	8	6	II
Robin Hood	Davis	Fy	2	10	5	II
Rollo's Wild Oat	Kummer	C	4	7	5	I
Romance	Sheldon	D	#	10	6	I
Romantic Age	Milne	C	2	5	4	II
Romeo and Jane	Carpenter	C	1	5	3	III
Rosary	Rose	D	3	5	4	II
Rosemary	Parker	D	3	6	4	II
Rose In Bloom	Ravold	C	1	7	8	III
Rose O'Plymouth Town	Dix-Sutherland	D	1	4	4	III
Rose of the Rancho	Belasco	D	3	22	9	I
Rose of the Southland	Short	C	1	4	6	III
Rosmersholm	Ibsen	D	3	4	2	I
Royal Family	Kaufman-Ferber	C	1	11	6	II
Rugged Road	Wayne-Sprague	D	1	9	7	III
R. U. R.	Capek	Md	1	13	4	I
Russet Mantle	Riggs	D	2	6	6	I
Ryerson Mystery	Phelps-Short	My	1	5	5	III
Sag Harbor	Herne	D	4	10	8	I
Sally and Company	Nicholson	C	2	5	9	II
Saturday's Children	Anderson	C	2	3	4	I
Scarecrow	Mackaye	D	2	11	5	I
Sap	Grew	C	1	4	3	II
Sap Runs High	Porter-White	C	1	5	9	II
Saturday Evening Ghost	Taggart	My	1	4	4	III
Saving Grace	Chambers	C	1	3	4	II
School for Scandal	Sheridan	C	#	13	5	I
Scrap of Paper	Simpson	C	2	6	6	III
Second Childhood	Covington	C	1	6	6	II
Second Fiddle	LePeltret	C	1	3	6	III
Second Man	Behrman	C	1	3	2	I
Second Mrs. Tanqueray	Pinero	D	3	7	4	I
Secret Service	Gillette	D	1	16	5	I
Sentimental Sarah	George	C	1	4	8	III
Servant In the House	Kennedy	D	1	5	2	I
Service for Two	Flavin	C	1	4	4	I
Seven Chances	Megrue	F	2	7	8	II
Seven Keys to Baldpate	Cohan	My	1	9	4	II
Seventeen	Tarkington	C	3	8	6	II
Shannons of Broadway	Gleason	C	1	18	6	II
Shavings	Phelps-Short	C	2	8	3	II
She Loves Me Not	Lindsay	C	#	18	7	I
Shenandoah	Howard	D	#	14	7	I
She Stoops to Conquer	Goldsmith	C	3	15	4	II
Shirt Sleeves	Burdette	C	1	12	9	III
Shore Acres	Herne	D	4	19	11	I
Show Off	Kelly	C	1	6	3	II
Silas Marner	Eliot-Ravold	D	1	10	7	I
Silas, the Chore Boy	Bernard	C	1	6	3	I
Silver Cord	Howard	D	1	2	3	I
Silver Tassie	O'Casey	Fy	4	19	4	I

Play	Author	Type	Sets	Men	Women	Grade
Sister Beatrice	Maeterlinck	Fu	1	2	10	I
Sittin' Pretty	Harris	C	1	14	0	III
Sis Perkins	Braun	F	1	4	6	III
Six Characters	Pirandello	Fy	1	#	#	I
Skidding	Rouverol	C	1	5	5	II
Skinner's Dress Suit	Dodge	C	2	6	5	II
Smilin Thru'	Martin	D	2	5	5	I
Snow-White and Seven Dwarfs	White	Fy	2	#	#	II
Some Call It Love	Ziegfeld	C	1	4	5	III
Solitaire Man	Spewacks	My	1	7	3	II
So This Is London	Goodrich	C	3	7	4	II
Sort of Prince	Brighouse	C	1	6	6	II
Something to Talk About	Doran	C	1	4	8	III
So You're from Missouri	Ziegfeld	F	1	5	5	III
Spider and the Fly	George	C	1	4	7	III
Speed	Braun	F	1	4	6	III
Speak for Yourself	Spence	C	1	3	7	III
Spooks	Sherman	My	1	7	4	II
Spring Dance	Barry	C	2	6	7	II
Springtime for Henry	Levy	C	1	2	2	II
Stop Thief	Moore	F	1	8	5	II
Squaring the Circle	Kataaev	F	1	7	5	II
St. Joan	Shaw	D	#	#	#	I
Step Out Jack	Osborne	C	3	12	5	III
Straight Thru the Door	Hodge	My	2	11	6	II
Strange Interlude	O'Neill	D	5	5	3	I
Strangers At Home	Divine	D	1	8	9	III
Street Scene	Rice	D	1	29	16	I
Strenuous Life	Tully	F	1	12	5	III
Strongheart	DeMille	D	3	17	5	II
Stubbornness of Geraldine	Fitch	C	2	10	12	I
Substitute for Sally	Doran	C	1	4	8	III
Success	Milne	C	3	9	4	I
Successful Calamity	Kummer	C	1	9	3	II
Such a Little Queen	Pollock	C	4	12	5	II
Suicide Specialist	Pierce	C	2	5	6	III
Summer Is A-Cumin In	Parker	C	1	5	6	II
Sun-Up	Vollmer	D	1	7	2	I
Swan	Molnar	C	1	9	8	II
Swappers	Loving	C	2	7	8	III
Sweetest Girl In Town	George	Mu	1	7	9	II
Sweet Lavender	Pinero	Md	2	7	4	II
Tailor Made Man	Smith	C	3	20	8	II
Take My Advice	Lester	C	1	5	3	II
Take My Tip	Dorfman	C	1	7	6	II
Take Off Those Whiskers	Spence	F	1	11	9	III
Taming of Tuffy	Jones	C	1	6	4	III
Tea for Three	Megrue	C	1	3	2	II
Tavern	Cohan	C	1	10	4	II
Teacher Was Right	Doran	C	1	4	8	III
Tell Me Your Troubles	Nicholson	C	2	8	4	II
Tell the Judge	Todd	F	1	5	3	III
That Ferguson Family	Chenery	C	1	5	5	II
That Orphan	Doran	C	1	5	9	III
That's the Ticket	Gibson	C	1	4	3	III
These Are Your Neighbors	Doran	C	1	6	8	III
Thief	Bernstein	C	3	5	2	I

Play	Author	Type	Sets	Men	Women	Grade
Their New Deal	Munbrun	D	1	0	9	III
Ten Minute Alibi	Armstrong	My	1	6	1	II
There's Always Juliet	Van Drutes	C	1	2	2	I
They All Want Something	Savage	C	1	8	6	II
They Will Grow Up	Short	C	1	4	6	III
Things	O'Ryan	C	1	2	8	III
Things That Count	Eyre	C	2	5	11	II
Third Degree	Klein	D	3	12	2	I
Thirteen Diamonds	Short	C	1	5	9	III
Thirteenth Chair	Veiller	My	1	10	7	II
Thirty Days	Hamilton	F	3	12	5	II
Thompson	Calderon-Hankin	C	2	5	5	II
Those Devoted Dapplebys	Wayne	C	1	7	4	III
Thirty-Nine East	Crothers	C	3	6	8	II
Three Cornered Moon	Tonkonog	C	1	5	4	II
Three Graces	Nicholson-Reed	C	1	8	5	III
Three Days of Gracie	Metcalfe	F	1	10	8	III
Three Live Ghosts	Isham-Marcin	C	1	6	4	II
Three Men On a Horse	Abbot	F	2	11	4	I
Three Strikes and Out	Braun	F	1	5	6	III
Three Taps At Twelve	Saunders	My	1	6	3	III
Three Wise Fools	Strong	C	1	11	2	II
Through the Keyhole	Davidson	C	1	4	4	III
Thunderbolt	Pinero	C	2	13	6	I
Tightwad	Keith	C	1	6	5	III
Tigerhouse	St. Clair	My	1	7	4	III
Tilly of Bloomsbury	Hay	C	2	9	7	II
Tin Hero	George	F	1	4	8	III
Tobacco Road	Kirkland	C	1	6	5	I
Toad of Toad Hall	Milne	Fy	#	19	8	I
Tomboy	Loving	C	1	5	9	III
Tomorrow and Tomorrow	Barry	D	1	5	6	I
Tom Sawyer	Kester	C	2	13	8	II
Tommy	Lindsay-Robinson	C	1	5	3	II
Tommy Tomorrow	Latham	C	2	12	13	III
Too Many Cooks	Craven	C	1	13	8	II
Too Much Johnson	Gillette	C	2	10	3	II
Topaze	Pagnol	C	2	19	5	I
Torch Bearers	Kelly	C	2	6	6	II
Torch Song	Nicholson	D	3	8	6	I
To the Ladies	Kaufman-Connelly	C	3	11	3	I
Tovarich	Duvall	C	3	9	7	I
Tower of Nesle	De Poncet	Md	6	16	3	I
Toymaker of Nuren.burg	Strong	D	#	15	3 Ex.	II
Tragedy of Nan	Masefield	D	1	8	5	I
Trelawny of the Wells	Pinero	C	2	14	9	I
Trial of Mary Dugan	Veiller	Md	1	20	7	I
Truth About Blaydes	Milne	C	1	4	4	I
Treasure Island	Goodman	D	8	24	1	I
Trials of Mary	Doran	C	1	4	8	III
True Adventure	Kaufman	C	2	4	2	II
Turn to the Right	Smith	C	3	9	5	II
Tweedles	Tarkington	C	1	5	4	II
Two Dicks	Springer	C	1	3	4	III
Two Mrs. Carrols	Vale	C	2	3	5	I
Two Mr. Weatherbys	Hankin	C	2	3	4	II

Play	Author	Type	Sets	Men	Women	Grade
Two Weeks Off	Nicholson	C	2	5	6	II
Unattainable	Maugham	F	1	3	4	I
Uncle Tom's Cabin	Aiken	D	#	15	6	I
Under Cover	Megrue	My	2	8	5	II
Unexpected Guest	Reese-White	C	1	7	4	III
Up Pops the Devil	Goodrich	C	1	10	5	I
Vagabond King	McCarthy	Mu	3	18	11 Ex.	I
Valley Farm	Tubbs	D	2	6	6	III
Valley Forge	Anderson	D	#	34	5	I
Vanity	Denny	C	1	5	6	III
Very Untruly Yours	Taggart	C	2	5	5	III
Vinegar Tree	Osborne	C	1	4	3	I
Volunteer Wife	Hunting-Marshall	C	1	4	6	III
Voysey Inheritance	Barker	D	2	10	8	I
Wait for Me	Braun	C	1	9	5	III
Wake Up Jonathan	Hughes-Rice	C	2	6	5	II
Warrior's Husband	Thompson	F	3	8	13	I
Wasp's Nest	Matthews	My	1	7	4	II
Waste	Barker	D	1	6	1	I
Watch Your Step	Savage	My	1	5	4	III
Way of the World	Congreve	C	3	12	8	I
Wedding Belle	Tobias	F	1	6	4	III
Wedding Bells	Field	C	1	5	4	II
Wedding Spells	Stone	F	1	5	7	III
Wednesday's Child	Atlas	D	7	11	5	I
Westward People	Rogers	C	1	4	3	III
What About Betty	Richardson	C	1	7	6	III
What a Relief	Loving	C	1	5	5	III
What Every Woman Knows	Barrie	C	2	5	3	I
What Happened to Jones	Broadhurst	C	1	7	6	II
When a Feller Needs a Friend	McMullen	C	1	5	5	III
When Knighthood Was In Flower	Kester	D	#	14	6	I
When Ladies Meet	Crothers	C	2	4	3	I
When's Your Birthday	Rouverol	C	1	6	4	II
Where Julia Rules	Ford-Duer	C	2	7	4	III
Where There's Fire	Gillam	C	1	5	7	III
Where There's a Willie	Applebud	C	3	7	7	III
Whippersnappers	Chenery	C	1	8	4	III
Whispering Gallery	Robinson-Marney	My	1	8	3	II
White Collars	Ellis	C	3	5	4	II
White Headed Boy	Robinson	C	1	5	7	I
White Elephant	Wright	C	1	6	4	III
Whitewashing Julia	Jones	C	3	15	4	I
Whispering Wires	McLaurin	My	1	9	5	II
Whole Town's Talking	Emerson-Loos	F	1	5	7	II
Who's Boss	Toler	F	1	4	6	III
Who's Crazy Now	Bell	C	1	3	8	III
Why Print That	Brumm	F	1	12	6	III
Why the Bachelor	McOwen	C	1	6	6	III
Why Smith Left Home	Broadhurst	C	2	5	7	II
Widow By Proxy	Cushing	C	1	4	5	II
Wild Duck	Ibsen	D	3	4	7	I
Window Panes	Printzlau	D	1	7	3	II
Wingless Victory	Anderson	D	2	5	4	I
Wind and the Rain	Hodge	D	1	6	3	III
Wings of the Morning	Burdette	C	4	6	10	II

Play	Author	Type	Sets	Men	Women	Grade
Wings Over Europe	Nichols-Browne	D	1	20	0	I
Wisdom Tooth	Connelly	My	5	19	10	I
Witching Hour	Thomas	D	1	12	4	I
Within the Law	Veiller	Md	4	15	5	I
Within These Walls	Bach	D	2	9	2	III
Within the Gates	O'Casey	Fy	#	#	#	I
Without Benefit of Relatives	Loving	C	1	5	7	III
Wives to Burn	McMullen	D	1	7	5	III
Woman of No Importance	Wilde	D	2	8	7	I
Wooden Slipper	Raphaelson	Fy	3	10	8	II
World Waits	Hummel	D	1	15	0	II
Would You Believe It	Doran	C	1	5	6	III
Wren	Tarkington	C	1	4	3	II
Wrong Mr. Wright	Broadhurst	F	1	7	4	II
Yankee King	Day	Fy	1	7	8	II
Yellow Jack	DeKruif	D	#	#	#	I
Yellow Jacket	Benrimo	Fy	#	17	12	I
You and I	Barry	C	1	4	3	II
Young America	Ballard	D	2	15	6	II
Young and Healthy	George	C	1	6	6	III
Younger Generation	Houghton	D	2	7	4	I
Young Heatherby	George	C	1	6	6	III
Youngest	Barry	C	2	4	5	II
Young Idea	Coward	C	2	7	7	I
Young Smitty	Warren	C	1	5	6	III
Young Woodley	Van Druten	D	2	7	2	I
Your Face Is Familiar	Todd	F	1	4	6	III
You're Telling Me	Braun	C	1	5	5	III
Your Uncle Dudley	Lindsay-Robinson	C	1	4	4	II
You Wouldn't Fool Me	Todd	F	1	5	5	III
You Never Can Tell	Shaw	C	2	6	6	I
Youth Comes Tripping	Holmes	C	1	6	3	III
Youth Shows the Way	Doran	C	1	3	7	III

APPENDIX B

BOOKS ON STAGE TECHNIQUE

Any of the following books may be purchased through *The Drama Book Shop Inc.*, 29 West 47th Street, New York.

Acting: Crafton and Royer.
Acting and Play Production: Andrews and Weirick.
Actors and the Art of Acting: George H. Lewis.
Amateur Actor, The: Frances MacKenzie.
American Dramatist, The: Montrose Moses.
Analysis of Play Production: W. T. Price.
Annals of the English Stage: John Doran.
Antoine and the Theatre Libre: S. M. Waxman.
Art of Acting, The: Coquelin.
Art of Directing Plays, The: D. C. Ashton.
Art of Play Production, The: John Dolman.
Art of Producing Pageants, The: Willard Bates.
Art of the Theatre, The: Sarah Bernhardt.
Art of the Theatre, The: Gordon Craig.
Art Theatre: Sheldon Cheney.
Attic Theatre: Arthur Haigh.
Behind the Scenes: John Sommerfield.
Book About the Theatre: Brander Matthews.
Book of Play Production: Milton Smith.
Chinese Theatre: A. E. Zucker.
Choosing the Play: Gertrude Johnson.
Commedia dell'Arte: Winifred Smith.
Continental Stagecraft: Kenneth MacGowan, Robert Jones.
Costuming the Play: Grimball and Wells.
Costumes and Scenery for Amateurs: Constance MacKay.
Craftsmanship of the One Act Play: Percival Wilde.
Development of the Theatre: Allardyce Nicoll.
Dramatic Technique: George Pierce Baker.
Dramatics for School and Community: Claude Wise.
Dramatic Opinions: George B. Shaw.
Dramatic Values: C. E. Montague.
Dramaturgie Als Wissenschaft: Hugo Dinger.
Dramatization: Simons-Orr.

Drawings for the Theatre: Robert Edmund Jones.
Earlier English Drama: Thomas W. Baldwin.
Elizabethan Stage: Sir E. K. Chambers.
English Theatre, The: Allardyce Nicoll.
Equipment for the School Theatre: Milton Smith.
Equipment for Stage Production: A. E. Krows.
European Theories of the Drama: Barrett Clark.
Exemplary Theatre: Granville-Barker.
Glossary of Stage Lighting: Stanley McCandless.
Guide to Longer Plays: Frank Shay.
Greek Theatre and Its Drama: Roy Flickinger.
Historic Costumes: Catherine Lester Morris.
Historic Costumes for the Stage: Lucy Barton.
History of Pantomine: R. J. Broadbent.
History of the Theatre in America: Arthur Hornblow.
History of Theatrical Art: Karl Manzius.
How to Produce Amateur Plays: Barrett Clark.
How to Produce Children's Plays: Constance D. MacKay.
How You Can Write Plays: Mark Swan.
Index to One Act Plays: Logasa and Vernoy.
Index to Plays 1800-1926: Ina Ten Eyck.
Irish Literature and Drama: Stephen Gwynn.
Kabuki (Japanese Theatre): Zoe Kincaid.
La Comedie Italienne: Pierre Duchartre.
Life of David Belasco: William Winter.
Little Country Theatre: Alfred Arvold.
Little Theatre Organization and Management: Alexander Dean.
Make-Up, The Art of: Helena Chalmers.
Make-Up: James Young.
Make-Up: John Baird.
Making the Little Theatre Pay: Oliver Hindsell.
Max Reinhardt and His Theatre: Oliver Saylor.
Masks and Faces: William Archer.
Medieval Stage: Sir F. X. Chambers.
Memories of a Manager: Daniel Frohman.
Mimes and Miming: Isabel Chisman and Gladys Wiles.
Modern Acting: Helena Chalmers.
Modern Drama: J. W. Marriott.
Modern Make-Up: Gall and Carter.
Modern Theatre: Irving Pichel.
Modern Theatre Construction: E. B. Kinsella.
Mrs. Fiske: Her Views on Actors and Acting: Wolcott.
My Life in Art: Constantin Stanislavsky.
My Life on the Stage: John Drew.
New Movement in the Theatre: Sheldon Cheney.
New Spirit in Drama and Dramatic Art: Huntley Carter.

Organized Theatre: St. John Ervine.
Path of the Modern Russian Stage: Alexander Bakshy.
Pattern Plays: E. C. Oakden and Mary Stuart.
Plays, Acting, and Music: Arthur Symonds.
Players Handbook: Samuel Selden.
Playwriting: William Archer.
Playwriting: Alfred Hennequin.
Playwriting for Profit: A. E. Krows.
Practical Stage Directing for Amateurs: Emerson Taylor.
Practical Theatre: Frank Shay.
Problems of the Actor: Louis Calvert.
Process of Play Production: Crafton and Royer.
Producing in Little Theatres: Clarence Stratton.
Producing School Plays: Ernest F. Dyer.
Russian Theatre Under the Revolution: Oliver Saylor.
Scene: Gordon Craig.
Scenery: Harold Helvensten.
Scenewright: Andre Smith.
Scene Technician's Manual: Philip Barber.
School Theatre, The: Roy Mitchell.
Secrets of Scene Painting and Stage Effects: VanDyke Brown.
Shakespeare from Betterton to Irving: George Odell.
Shakespearean Playhouse: Ashley Thorndyke.
So You're Writing a Play: Clayton Hamilton.
Stage Antiquities: James Allen.
Stage Costuming: Agnes Young.
Stage Decorations: Sheldon Cheney.
Stage Is Set, The: Lee Simonson.
Stage Lighting: C. H. Ridge.
Story of the Theatre, The: Glenn Hughes.
Studies in Stagecraft: Clayton Hamilton.
Technique of the Drama: Gustav Freytag.
Technique of Dramatic Art: Halliam Bosworth.
Theatre Advancing: Gordon Craig.
Theatre Lighting: Louis Hartman.
Theatre Lighting, Past and Present: Ward Leonard Electric Co.
Theatre Management: E. C. Stanton.
Theatre and the World, The: J. T. Grein.
Theatre of Today: Hiram Moderwell.
Theatre of Tomorrow: Kenneth MacGowan.
Theatre Practice: Stark Young.
Theatre Through the Stage Door: David Belasco.
Theatron: Clarence Stratton.
Theory of the Theatre: Clayton Hamilton.
Theory of the Theatre: Walter P. Eaton.
Thirty-Six Dramatic Situations: Polti.

The Theatre (3,000 Years of Drama, Acting, Stagecraft): Sheldon
Cheney.

Towards a New Theatre: Gordon Craig.

Training for the Stage: Arthur Hornblow.

Twentieth Century Theatre: William Lyon Phelps.

APPENDIX C

SUPPLY HOUSES

The Directory does not pretend to be complete. The information listed here was gathered from catalogues, from personal dealings, and from advertising in trade magazines.

COSTUMES AND MATERIALS

Arrow Textile Company, 1123 Broadway, New York City.
Brooks Costume and Uniform Company, 1437 Broadway, N. Y. C.
Dazian's Inc., 142 West 44th Street, New York City.
Eaves Costume Company, 110 West 46th Street, New York City.
Fechheimer Bros., Cincinnati, Ohio.
Martin Giesen, St. Paul, Minnesota.
C. H. Haentze, 244 S. 11th St., Philadelphia, Penn.
Hooker-Howe Company, Haverhill, Massachusetts.
Theo. Lieben & Son, Omaha, Nebraska.
Lowell Costume Company, Lowell, Massachusetts.
Malabar Costumes, Winnipeg, Manitoba.
Minneapolis Costume Company, Minneapolis, Minnesota.
New York Costume Co., 75 West Lake Street, Chicago.
Richards Costume Co., 630 N. High Street, Columbus, Ohio.
Paine Publishing Company, Dayton, Ohio.
Fritz Schoultz Co., 58 West Lake Street, Chicago.
Tams, 318 West 22nd Street, New York City.
Van Horn & Son, 12th and Chestnut Sts., Philadelphia.
Waas & Sons, Philadelphia.
Western Costume Corp., 5335 Melrose Ave., Hollywood, Calif.

LIGHTING EQUIPMENT

Acetol Products Co., 21 Spruce St., New York City.
Frank Adams Electric Co., 3650 Windsor Place, St. Louis, Mo.
Brenkert Light Projection Co., 7348 St. Aubin Ave., Detroit, Mich.
Century Lighting Co., 351 West 52nd Street, New York City.
Chicago Cinema Equipment Co., 802 S. Tripp St., Chicago, Ill.
Chicago Stage Lighting Co., 112 N. LaSalle St., Chicago, Ill.
Kliegl Bros., 321 West 50th St., New York City

Peter Clark Inc., 534 West 30th St., New York City.
Pevear Color Specialty Co., 71 Brimmer Street, Boston, Mass.
Rosco Laboratories, 131 Third Place, Brooklyn, N. Y.
Claude Seaman, 316 East 12th St., Los Angeles, Calif.
Trumbull Electric Co., Plainville, Conn.
Ward Leonard Electric Co., Mount Vernon, N. Y.

MAKE-UP AND WIGS

O. F. Berner, 107 West 46th Street, New York City.
A. M. Busch, 228 S. 11th Street, Philadelphia, Pa.
Max Factor, 326 S. Hill Street, Los Angeles, Calif.
Henry C. Miner, 12 East 12th Street, New York City.
M. Stein Cosmetic Co., 430 Broome Street, New York City.
Funk Wig Company, 36 State Street, Chicago, Ill.
Van Horn & Sons, Philadelphia, Pa.
Waas & Sons, Philadelphia, Pa.

PLAY PUBLISHERS AND AGENTS

American Play Company, 451 Broadway, New York City.
D. Appleton Company, 35 West 32nd Street, New York City.
Atlantic Monthly Press, Boston, Mass.
Walter Baker, 178 Tremont Street, Boston, Mass.
A. S. Barnes & Co., 65 West 45th Street, New York City.
Banner Play Bureau, 111 Ellis Street, San Francisco, Calif.
Boni & Liveright, 61 West 48th Street, New York City.
Brentano's, 1 West 47th Street, New York City.
Century Play Company, 1440 Broadway, New York City.
Century Company, 353 Fourth Avenue, New York City.
Columbia University Press, 2960 Broadway. New York City.
F. S. Crofts Company, 66 Fifth Avenue, New York City.
T. S. Dennison Company, 623 S. Wabash, Chicago, Ill.
Drama Book Shop, 29 West 47th Street, New York City.
Dodd, Mead, & Co., 443 Fourth Avenue, New York City.
George H. Doran & Co., 681 Fifth Avenue, New York City.
Dramatic Publishing Co., 542 S. Dearborn, Chicago, Ill.
E. P. Dutton, 681 Fifth Avenue, New York City.
Fitzgerald Publishing Co., 14 E. 38th Street, New York City.
Samuel French, 25 West 45th Street, New York City.
Eldridge Entertainment House, Franklin, Ohio.
Willis N. Bugbee, Syracuse, New York.
Harcourt Brace Co., 383 Madison Avenue, New York City.
Harper & Bros., 49 East 33rd Street, New York City.
Harvard University Press, 12 Randall Hall, Cambridge, Mass.
Henry Holt & Co., 1 Park Ave., New York City.
Houghton Mifflin Co., 2 Park St., Boston, Mass.
Ivan-Bloom-Hardin Co., Des Moines, Iowa.

International Play Bureau, San Francisco, Calif.
Alice Kauser, 1402 Broadway, New York City.
Alfred A. Knopf, 730 Fifth Avenue, New York City.
Little, Brown & Co., Boston, Mass.
Longmans, Green & Co., 114 Fifth Ave., New York City.
Macmillan Company, 60 Fifth Avenue, New York City.
Thomas Nelson and Sons, 381 Fourth Avenue, New York City.
Northwestern Press, Minneapolis, Minnesota.
Mitchell Kennerly, 32 West 38th St., New York City.
Row, Patterson Co., Evanston, Illinois.
Charles Scribner's Sons, 597 Fifth Avenue, New York City.
Simon & Schuster, 37 West 57th Street, New York City.
Frederick A. Stokes, 443 Fourth Avenue, New York City.
Shubert Theatre Co., 1416 Broadway, New York City.
Theatre Arts, Inc., 119 West 57th Street, New York City.
University of Washington Bookstore, Seattle, Washington.
Harold Vinal, 526 Fifth Avenue, New York City.
Woman's Press, 600 Lexington Avenue, New York City.

SCENERY, DRAPERIES, FABRICS

Beaumont Studios, 443 West 47th Street, New York City.
William Beck & Sons, 1117 Vine Street, Cincinnati, Ohio.
Robert Bergman, 142 West 39th Street, New York City.
Calkins, 935 S. Broadway, New York City.
Robert Carson Scenic Studio, 1507 N. Clark St., Chicago, Ill.
Curran & Craig, Boston, Mass.
Devereux Studios, 80 West 40th Street, New York City.
Theodore Kahn, 155 West 29th Street, New York City.
Mountain State Scenic Studio, Denver, Colorado.
Novelty Scenic Studios, 342 West 41st St., New York City.
Schell Scenic Studios, Columbus, Ohio.
Cleon Throckmorton, 102 West 3rd St., New York City.
Vail Construction Co., 320 West 24th St., New York City.
I. Weiss & Sons, 508 West 43rd St., New York City.
Tiffin Scenic Studios, Tiffin, Ohio.

ART SUPPLIES

Aljo Manufacturing Co., 168 West 22nd Street, New York City.
Primatic Art Co., 303 Fifth Avenue, New York City.
Erwin M. Reibe Co., 105 East 59th Street, New York City.

HARDWARE

Peter Clark, 544 West 30th Street, New York City.
J. R. Clancy, Syracuse, New York.
United Theatre Equipment, Boston, Mass.

TICKETS

Argus Ticket Company, 348 N. Ashland Avenue, Chicago, Ill.
Elliot Ticket Company, Canal and Vestry Sts., New York City.
Globe Ticket Company, N. 12th Street, Philadelphia, Pa.
International Ticket Company, 50 Grafton Ave., Newark, N. J.
Trimont Press, 113 Albany, New York.
World Ticket and Supply Co., 1600 Broadway, New York City.

SCHOOLS OF THE THEATRE

Alviene School of the Theatre, 349 W. 85th St., New York City.
Actor's Workshop, 349 W. 86th St., New York City.
American Academy of Dramatic Art, Carnegie Hall, New York
   City.
American Laboratory Theatre, 145 East 45th St., New York City.
Fanny Bradshaw, 136 East 57th Street, New York City.
Boston Repertoire Theatre, Boston, Mass.
Carnegie Institute of Technology, Pittsburgh, Pa.
Chicago School of Dramatic Arts, Fine Arts Bldg., Chicago, Ill.
Columbia College of Expression, 616 S. Michigan Ave., Chicago,
   Ill.
Cornish School, Seattle, Washington.
Drama Teachers' Summer School, Berkeley, Calif.
Eastman School, Rochester, N. Y.
Feagin Dramatic School, Carnegie Hall, New York City.
John Gallishaw School, 36 East 40th Street, New York City.
Gloucester School, Rocky Neck, Gloucester, Mass.
Goodman Theatre, Arts Institute, Chicago, Ill.
Theodora Irvine Studio, 310 West 73rd St., New York City.
Ithaca College, Ithaca, New York.
Maria Ouspenskaya, 27 West 67th Street, New York City.
New York School, 139 West 5th Street, New York City.
School of the Theatre, Savannah, Ga.

Many universities now offer thorough training in playwriting, acting, and producing. This is perhaps the best
type of training, as it couples broad education with specialized instruction in the stage arts.